PENGUI

PERFECT BLOOD PRESSURE

Dr David Lovell-Smith was born in Christchurch, New Zealand, in 1951. Having twice secured a competitive and sought-after place at Otago Medical School he declined both times, first in favour of completing a Bachelor of Arts in music and philosophy, and the second time to train as a teacher of Transcendental Meditation. He now regards these as the best preparation he could have had for the study of medicine. He graduated MB ChB in 1978 and since 1982 has run a general medical practice in Christchurch. He is a Senior Clinical Lecturer with the Department of General Practice of the Christchurch School of Medicine and is currently completing a Masters degree in General Practice through Otago University.

Dr Lovell-Smith is a leading exponent of the Vedic Approach to Health as brought to light by Maharishi Mahesh Yogi. As President of the Maharishi Medical Association of New Zealand he has fostered this approach in the medical setting throughout New Zealand. He has lectured widely on the subject and has written about it in the *New Zealand Medical Journal, New Zealand Family Physician* and *New Zealand GP*. He has travelled extensively, his studies having taken him many times to India, Europe and the United States.

In keeping with his desire to promote whole-person medicine, Dr Lovell-Smith has been vocal in alerting the public to the dangers of genetically engineered food.

Dr Lovell-Smith is married with three teenage children. His leisure activities include tramping (hiking), sailing, tennis and playing chamber music with his friends. He has made a harpsichord.

*To my parents, Anne Lovell-Smith,
eternal champion of perfection,
and Hugh Lovell-Smith, physician,
who approached perfection in his
gentle compassionate care.*

PERFECT BLOOD PRESSURE
Naturally

Dr David Lovell-Smith
BA, MBChB, FRNZCGP

PENGUIN BOOKS

PENGUIN BOOKS

Penguin Books (NZ) Ltd, cnr Airborne and Rosedale Roads, Albany,
Auckland 1310, New Zealand
Penguin Books Ltd, 27 Wrights Lane, London W8 5TZ, England
Penguin Putnam Inc, 375 Hudson Street, New York, NY 10014, United States
Penguin Books Australia Ltd, 487 Maroondah Highway, Ringwood,
Australia 3134
Penguin Books Canada Ltd, 10 Alcorn Avenue, Toronto, Ontario,
Canada M4V 3B2
Penguin Books (South Africa) Pty Ltd, 5 Watkins Street, Denver Ext 4, 2094, South Africa
Penguin Books India (P) Ltd, 11, Community Centre, Panchsheel Park,
New Delhi 110 017, India

Penguin Books Ltd, Registered Offices: Harmondsworth, Middlesex, England

First published by Penguin Books (NZ) Ltd, 2001

3 5 7 9 10 8 6 4 2

Copyright © David Lovell-Smith, 2001

The right of David Lovell-Smith to be identified as the author of this work in terms of
section 96 of the Copyright Act 1994 is hereby asserted.

Illustrations by Penelope Donovan
Designed by Mary Egan
Typeset by Egan-Reid Ltd
Printed in Australia by McPherson's Printing Group, Maryborough

ISBN 0 14 029887 8

All patient names in this book are fictitious
and bear no relation to any persons, living or dead.

CONTENTS

A Word to the Wise

The information provided in this book is for your better health. The scientific discoveries reported here can transform human health and health care. Long-term studies show that we can significantly improve our health and reduce the load on our over-stressed health care system. I am convinced that everyone should be aware of the concepts and research described in this book. That does not mean, however, that people who read this book should try to become medical experts on their own. Nothing in this book is meant to replace the advice of a physician. Any decision you make involving the treatment of an illness should include input from your medical doctor. Do not change medication without professional advice, or make changes to your diet if you are seriously ill or on medication without first consulting your doctor. It *is* possible to have the best of both worlds.

Preface

Scientific medicine is an international discipline whose borders transcend national boundaries. In 1997 I had the pleasure of conducting a lecture tour of New Zealand during which Dr David Lovell-Smith introduced me to medical leaders and professional groups throughout the country. Dr Lovell-Smith has for thirty years been in the vanguard of an international community of doctors who have discovered the practical wisdom of the Vedic system of health as brought to light by Maharishi Mahesh Yogi. This cadre of health professionals includes members from all sectors of the medical work-force. My own work as clinical practitioner and research pathologist led me to study the Vedic herbal preparations for their anti-oxidant and other important effects. This, and the work of my colleagues around the world, provides strong evidence that Maharishi's Vedic Approach to Health is invaluable in addressing the risk factors for heart disease, including hypertension. A glance at the medical literature shows that hypertension is topical. Heart disease is our number one killer, and the medical profession is desperate for answers. The techniques of Maharishi's Vedic Approach to Health have been shown to be effective. They cannot be ignored.

Dr Lovell-Smith's thoughtful analysis of the complex field of hypertension is a major contribution that comes out of his long experience at the coalface of medicine. As a community doctor he is dealing with people, their feelings, their relationships, their lives. He sees the devastating effects that a stroke or heart attack has on a patient, the patient's family and his community. He sees first-hand the troubling, sometimes dangerous effects of drugs. The marked improvements in health and vitality that can follow use of the techniques from Maharishi's Vedic Approach to Health are a daily inspiration to him.

You may have normal blood pressure, but is it perfect? Are you at risk? We should all read this important, very timely book.

Hari Sharma, MD
Emeritus Professor of Pathology
The Ohio State University College of Medicine
Columbus, Ohio

Introduction

In writing this book my intention is to give hope and encouragement to the many people who have been diagnosed as suffering from 'hypertension' and who feel intuitively that there is something deeply wrong about accepting a life-time sentence of drug taking. If you are in that situation, then take heart. There is a lot more to the story of hypertension than most patients are ever told. You can do a great deal to help yourself without resorting to drugs.

I run a fairly standard kind of medical practice. I listen to people's chests, sew up their cut fingers and try to keep up to date with medical trends. Yet the reader will find that I am disenchanted with much of the current medical management of hypertension. My attitude may owe much to the fact that before entering medical school I was lucky enough to be able to put medicine on hold and spend a few years completing an arts degree, during which I became absorbed in the study of philosophy. It was in those early lectures and tutorials that I became aware of the vast compass of Western and Eastern thought. It became clear to me that our day-to-day decisions, and those of the professionals on whom we depend, are underpinned by thousands of other people's thoughts and opinions, all mixed up together, some evident and some, especially those that come to us from our past, all but buried in our collective consciousness.

Realising that I and those around me were unwittingly accepting a rag-bag of ideas 'second-hand' alerted me to tease out and question the various assumptions and approximations that had been made on my behalf. On entering medical school, I found plenty of material on which to exercise this frame of mind!

I even considered joining the New Zealand Skeptics' Society. While my attitude should have qualified me for immediate membership, I was sceptical of their scepticism, inclining to the view that it was merely a front for a rather materialistic philosophy. So being sceptical of the Skeptics, I was not sure whether I would be admitted to their Society!

In any case it did not seem sufficient to be simply sceptical. I was looking for knowledge that I would find satisfying, that, rather than being a mish-mash of notions, would have an internal consistency and the ability to withstand scrutiny. In my youthful idealism I wanted knowledge that could deal with the great questions and bring with it the power to do good for the world.

Thus it was that having completed the arts degree I was even more fortunate to again put medical studies aside and spend a year overseas following up my interest in Eastern epistemology. I had read with great interest about the wisdom of ancient cultures, for example, Chinese, Tibetan and Indian. Hatha Yoga was becoming popular and, along with many of my student friends, I had learned Transcendental Meditation. I was particularly eager to know about its roots in the ancient Vedic knowledge of India.

Readers might notice that my critical attitude seems to melt in the second and third sections of the book, as indeed it does. In those crucial years before entering the 'lock-step' routine of medical school, I realised that I had stumbled on a system of knowledge that could survive my more-than-ordinary scepticism. Indeed, it has survived the scrutiny of many generations over thousands of years. It seems well able to meet the challenge of modern scientific inspection.

I must therefore at the outset declare my position, which is now well and truly in favour of the Vedic Approach to Health, as it has been brought to light by the Indian sage and scholar Maharishi Mahesh Yogi.

Maharishi's Vedic Approach to Health is a cornucopia of practical lifestyle, dietary and other techniques, which, among their many other health benefits, get to the root not only of the problem of high blood pressure, but also of a vast array of other medical conditions and problems of living.

The most important among the programmes of Maharishi's Vedic Approach to Health is the technique of Transcendental Meditation. The unique process of transcending thought that occurs when Transcendental Meditation is practised should not be confused with other forms of meditation, most of which are difficult if not downright impossible. Transcendental Meditation, by contrast, is easy and effective. Because it is unique I refer to it specifically throughout the book, rather than using the generic term 'meditation'. There is no doubt in my mind that I have done the most service for my patients by helping them to learn this delicate yet simple skill. Maharishi's Vedic Approach to Health may seem far removed from the everyday business of getting one's blood pressure down. There is still a lamentable gap between public perception and the reality of Maharishi's colossal contribution in the field of health. I hope readers will suspend judgement until the book has been read, for the truth is that Maharishi's work in bringing to light the essence of the Vedic knowledge from India is of inestimable value.

It is encouraging to see the high degree of medical and research interest now in Maharishi's Vedic Approach to Health, with over 600 studies having been performed on Transcendental Meditation, many thousands of doctors practising the technique and many more recommending it to their patients.

This is a system of health that not only treats disease but also helps us become truly healthy. While it will not be possible to take you through the many twists and turns of thought I encountered along the path, I hope that the pages that follow will give you some insight into the process that allowed me to finally drop my scepticism and become an enthusiast.

Why should you need to know more about Maharishi's Vedic Approach to Health? Because it works. If you have high blood pressure, then it could be helping you, safely and effectively. Perhaps you have normal blood pressure, but is it perfect? There is a difference as I will attempt to show.

PART ONE

The 'Silent Killer'

ONE

A Difficult Day for Cresswell Jones

It has been an awkward day for Cresswell Jones, newly appointed accountant with Frawley, Frawley, Frawley, Frampton and Quelch. Daphne, Cresswell's daughter, has run through her money, dropped out of university, and turned up to live in the caravan behind the house. His llama, an investment for its valuable fibre (and never a very predictable beast at the best of times), has bitten into the electricity supply Jones had rigged to the caravan. Badly shaken, it has rampaged wildly through Jones' glasshouse full of investment asparagus. Windows have been shattered to say nothing of Jones' nerves.

Frawley, Frawley, etc. have asked him to take a medical examination, his first in five years. While hurrying to his doctor's rooms, Jones grabs his briefcase wildly out of the car, slams the car door, locks his keys inside, and, becoming aware of a constriction around his throat, realises he has jammed his tie in the door!

When he finally arrives at the surgery Jones' tension is almost palpable.

The doctor places a cuff around Jones' rather flabby arm. He palpates the brachial artery, then holds his stethoscope against it. He pumps away at the bulb of the sphygmomanometer, and the cuff inflates. The velcro pulls away slightly, making a tearing sound. The arm feels slightly engorged and uncomfortable. Jones wonders whether any damage is being

*done to his delicate capillaries by such an unnatural practice. The doctor
says nothing, but frowns a little and repeats the measurement while
peering intently at the mercury as it slides erratically down the glass tube
of the sphygmomanometer. 'Hmm . . .160 over 100,' he mutters.*

'How is it doctor?' asks Jones anxiously.

*'Ah, well, Jones, I'm afraid your blood pressure is a little high. Quite
high, in fact. About 160 over 100. There's a danger you could have a stroke
or a heart attack. I'm going to run a few tests, then if your blood pressure
remains high I will need to prescribe some tablets for you to take twice a
day. I must ask you not to miss any doses—that's very important.'*

'Er, yes, doctor. Whatever you say.'

*(Thinks) But I feel OK! I'm not sick! I've got by without them so far.
What's wrong with me suddenly!*

*'You've probably got hypertension, you see. If so, you will need to take
pills for the rest of your life.'*

Good grief! Every day for the rest of my life!

Wrenched from the reassuringly familiar chaos of professional and
family life, Cresswell Jones suddenly confronts frailty, uncertainty and
the prospect of his own mortality. Called the 'silent killer' because of its dark
association with fatal heart attacks and strokes, high blood pressure, alias hypertension, affects about one out of five of all people aged between 15 and 65 in
industrialised countries. It looks as if Cresswell has joined them. Cresswell has
enlisted among the ranks of those millions of people worldwide—about 43
million in the United States alone—who carry the label 'hypertensive'.

> Called the 'silent killer' because of its dark association with fatal heart attacks and strokes, high blood pressure, alias hypertension, affects about one out of five of all people aged between 15 and 65 . . .

Hypertension works quietly—there are virtually no symptoms.
Without having had his blood pressure measured, Cresswell would
have been completely unaware of its presence.

He's lucky in that respect. But what should he do? What
should you do, if you were to find yourself in the same boat?

Does Cresswell have any options?

Until a few years ago, the official wisdom was 'no'. Cresswell has no choice. If the tests show that he has essential hypertension (hypertension for which there is no correctable physical cause), then for his own safety, Cresswell must remain on medication for the remainder of his days.

This is not true. It never was true. Yet there are powerful interests that even today would have you still believe it.

You do have options, very good ones, and this book sets out to tell you about them. We will first look at the story behind Cresswell Jones' consultation—there is more to it than one might think. We will then step back from the confusing biomedical world-view that gave birth to hypertension, and consider a much broader frame of reference. From this deeper understanding we will see that decisions have been made on your behalf. These decisions are based on assumptions that you might well want to question. I hope you will quickly gain the confidence to choose your own preferred options.

On the surface, Cresswell's visit to the doctor seems straight-forward. A man goes to his doctor, the doctor finds something wrong and prescribes a remedy. What could be more simple than that? Yet there are powerful undercurrents to this interchange that modify the behaviour of its protagonists.

Cresswell feels pressure to take his doctor's advice. After all, his doctor has trained for many years in a respected profession. So Cresswell tends not to think for himself.

Cresswell's doctor feels pressure to come up with a diagnosis. The patient wants to know exactly what is wrong, and the doctor wants to be able to tell him, clearly and precisely.

His doctor also feels pressure to follow the tenets of his profession. He wants to do just what any other doctor would do in that situation. Otherwise is he really a doctor? So the doctor tends to think not only about Cresswell, but also about his peers, and what they would think of him.

And his peers? As a group, doctors are under pressure to base their decisions on what they call 'best evidence'. In practice, best evidence turns out to be statistical evidence, based on epidemiological studies.

Epidemiology has its basis in the idea that environmental factors can influence the occurrence of a disease. This is a useful line of enquiry, yet it is important to remember that epidemiological studies deal with populations rather than individuals.

Populations may be studied descriptively, in which measurements are simply made on a given population, to find, say, the average blood pressure, or they may be analytical 'cohort' studies in which a group of people are followed over time, their exposure to a potential cause of disease (for example, smoking) is assessed and the incidence of disease among those who were exposed is compared with those who were not exposed. In descriptive and analytical studies nature is allowed to take its course—the experimenter observes, but does not interfere. In experimental studies, the 'gold standard' among which is the randomised controlled trial (RCT), the experimenter attempts to 'put nature to the test'. In an RCT, people are randomly assigned either to a group that receives active therapy, such as a drug, or to one that receives 'dummy' therapy, such as sugar pills. One group is then compared against the other.

People are different from one another. What is good for 'Mr Average' may not be good for Cresswell Jones.

Whether descriptive, analytical or experimental, the target of an epidemiological study is a human population, or group. What is good for a group is not necessarily good for an individual. People are different from one another. What is good for 'Mr Average' may not be good for Cresswell Jones. Already forces are coming into play that are causing this consultation to drift away from Cresswell.

Nevertheless, there is pressure to do *something*. While we do not know for sure what will happen to Cresswell, we do know that if he does have hypertension, then he is playing with loaded dice. Statistically speaking, based on the 'best evidence', his doctor is right. Cresswell has a greater risk of heart attack (death of heart tissue), heart failure (loss of the heart's ability to pump properly), kidney failure and stroke (death of brain tissue). Doing nothing is therefore not a good option.

There is one final pressure. The medical profession is assiduously wooed by the makers of pharmaceutical medication. Most of the 'best evidence' happens to be all about the use of drugs. The companies that supply pharmaceutical agents often supply the money to run the studies that produce the evidence. These companies are, quite understandably, under pressure to make a profit for their shareholders, and, being in business, they know all about marketing.

There are many ways to bring blood pressure down. The dominance of the pharmaceutical presence in medicine has skewed the attention of the profession away from other methods. I am not suggesting non-pharmacological methods are not recognised, but the very words used to describe them indicate that the emphasis is actually on pharmacology. Otherwise why call them 'non-pharmacological'? In my experience, 'non-pharmacological methods' tend to be relegated by the profession to the status of a poor cousin who, while recognised, receives very little funding and to whom lip service tends to be paid.

Cresswell wants to stay healthy and well. That is Cresswell's aim. Cresswell probably assumes that this is the sole aim of everyone else who is involved in his care. But is it? In fact, each of the parties involved has its own set of goals.

This is not to say that there is an organised 'conspiracy' going on here. It just happens that those who work in the world of medicine, in the world of research and in the world of business

Their interests may not always be in the best interests of you, the patient, a unique and special person.

have interests of their own. Their interests may not always be in the best interests of you, the patient, a unique and special person. It is good to understand this. Then you are in a position to make your own decisions.

The doctor's goals are actually mixed, although he probably doesn't realise this. He wants to help Cresswell as much as he can, but, as we have seen, he also wants to be a 'good doctor' and follow the professional line. He feels the two goals come to the same thing, so he experiences no discomfort in 'doing what any other doctor would do in the circumstances'. As we shall see in later chapters, these two goals may not come to the same thing at all. They may be widely divergent.

The profession is influenced by habit, the constraints of its own hidden assumptions and the goals of other interested parties.

The doctor has another goal, which is to find a label for his patient. He needs to round off each consultation in a clearcut and satisfying manner, preferably within ten to fifteen minutes. For this he would be greatly helped by having a diagnosis, or at least a clear step towards gaining one. If his patient can walk out with a provisional diagnosis, a form for some tests and a prescription for a remedy, then both patient and doctor feel that money has been well spent and good service given. Strangely enough, as we shall see, the urge to label may not always be in the best interest of the patient.

Those medical researchers, the epidemiologists, who do the large-scale population studies have a goal that may, again surprisingly, be quite a long way removed from Cresswell's goal. Their goal is to find ways to lower the incidence of sickness and death in a population. It is also the goal of those who make decisions about public funding, such as government Health Ministers. They ask questions like: 'Can we lower the incidence of heart attacks, heart failure and strokes in our country, by giving drug x, or diet x to all the hypertensives that live in this country?' Their answers give us excellent information about populations, but as we have mentioned, these answers cannot be applied to individuals. Let me give you an extreme illustration. Putting an antihypertensive medication into the tap water would almost certainly lower the incidence of strokes, heart failure and heart attacks in a city. It would achieve the goal of the epidemiologist very effectively. But it would not be good for the majority of individuals, who did not need the drug and may suffer from its side-effects. Unfortunately, as we shall see, the glittering goal of bringing the death rate down—saving lives—has blinded the profession, if not to the extent that it is tipping drugs into the town water supplies of the world, then at least to the unnecessary and sometimes extreme overuse of drugs.

Similarly, banning the sale of salt and high-fat foods would undoubtedly lower the incidence of strokes and heart attacks in the population as a whole. But would it help Cresswell? Epidemiologists have enthusiastically enjoined us all to eat almost no salt and cut back on high-fat foods. This helps some people and just makes others feel miserable. It is probably not necessary for everyone to follow such a strict regime and unfortunately it has put some people off trying to find alternative ways to bring their blood pressure down. To them, it just seems easier, in the end, to take the pills.

The drug companies are in the market to make a profit. Their goal is to sell plenty of drugs. If this were also to fulfil Cresswell's goal of staying healthy there would be no problem. However, these two goals are also often very far apart.

Hypertension is big business, not only for these companies but for doctors, laboratories and hospitals as well. In the United States, the annual cost for medications, visits to the doctor and laboratory tests associated with the detection and treatment of hypertension was reported in 1991 to exceed $10 billion.[1]

Whose goal is the most important? Cresswell's, isn't it? Or if you are in Cresswell's situation, then yours.

Your goal is to stay healthy and well. There are many ways you can do this.

Your goal is to stay healthy and well. There are many ways you can do this. I will describe some very useful methods in the pages that follow. But first let me tell you about Brad, because he lowered his blood pressure almost by accident. I met Brad many years ago when I was just starting out in general practice. In his late fifties, in a high-stress occupation, Brad worked extremely conscientiously. His face carried the typically worn expression of one who has rather a large part to play in a rather small business. For years, every three months, I examined him, asked him how he was getting along, and duly prescribed his blood pressure tablets. Provided he took the tablets, Brad's blood pressure was reasonably well controlled, with systolic levels usually about 130 mm Hg and diastolic levels of about 85 mm Hg.

One day, though, I noticed that Brad was looking unusually relaxed and carefree. He mentioned rather sheepishly that he was late in getting his pills this time. In fact he had not taken any for three weeks! I measured his blood pressure and noticed the pressure was still the same: 130/85 mm Hg! When I commented on this, Brad smiled and said, 'Well since I retired two weeks ago, I have done just exactly what

I felt like doing. I have played a lot of golf and I'm feeling just great!'

I was intrigued and decided not to give Brad any more tablets, but just monitor his blood pressure levels. For over fifteen years Brad has not needed a single tablet! For safety's sake I still measure his blood pressure every three months, but it seems that all Brad needed for a cure was to get out of his demanding and stressful job!

It was after meeting Brad that I began to question whether hypertension was quite the sinister demon that my training had led me to believe. Silent killer? Yes, the statistics certainly are there. But if something as simple as retirement and a few good games of golf could cause this ogre to disappear, then perhaps the villain is more vulnerable than we thought.

Powerful forces, including long-held habits, peer pressure among doctors and strong commercial interests are at work. Could it be that we have been caught up in a kind of *danse macabre*? I began to imagine a grotesque *folie à trois*, in which doctor, patient and drug manufacturer circle each other. The patient follows the doctor, who in turn takes his steps from the drug supplier who does his research on the patient, which convinces the doctor to further convince the patient to follow the doctor, who follows the supplier . . . Perhaps we could step out of this dance?

Dierdre did. Dierdre is a busy fifty-year-old businesswoman, married with three grown-up children. Her blood pressure problems started twenty-five years ago when she first became pregnant. After pregnancy her body never seemed fully to return to its former balanced state. Over the years her doctors had tried her on four different kinds of blood pressure pills. Taking these made her feel tired and 'not herself', but year after year she dutifully swallowed her medicine three times every day. Even taking the drugs, her blood pressure proved difficult to bring into the normal range, most readings being obstinately high. When Dierdre became a patient in my practice, instead of simply repeating her prescription, I gave her some lifestyle and dietary advice, together with a herbal preparation. These were based on Maharishi's Vedic Approach to Health. Her blood pressure readings fell consistently into the normal range within a few days. Eleven years later her blood pressure remains ideal, and she takes no pills at all, apart from a very small dose of the herbal preparation each day. How did she feel about this? 'I am myself again.'

One thing I have noticed in helping patients who have discovered that their blood pressure is too high, is that they have lots of questions. What exactly is hypertension? How do you know I've got it? What caused this? A discovery such as this radically alters our perception of ourselves, perhaps alters our lives, so these questions are natural. If you are in this situation, then some questions you will think to ask, others you probably forget or you may feel shy to ask them of a busy professional. Some will be barely articulated, being more of a feeling of discontent—a kind of intuition that 'there's something not quite right here somehow'.

So in the next chapter of this book I have tried to remember all the questions that patients have asked me. I will attempt to answer them. Sometimes the answers will take us far from the usual language of medicine, for although there are the glib replies, the kind that appear in the 'So You Have Hypertension' brochures that are to be found in doctors' waiting rooms, the real answers go beyond this. They extend into the very philosophy of our culture and beyond. Our answers will take us to the ancient Greeks and beyond—deep into the five-thousand-year-old Vedic tradition.

TWO

Help! What's Happening?

Cresswell Jones (remember him? llamas? glasshouses?) has been quietly digesting the unpalatable truth that his blood pressure readings taken over a number of weeks are consistently high. His systolic pressures have been in the range 150–180 mm Hg and his diastolic pressures 95–110 mm Hg. He has been told that he has mild to moderate hypertension. He has declined his doctor's recommendation to start tablets immediately. The more he thinks about his situation, the more questions he seems to have. How can he be sick when he feels so well? What is the cause of all this? Some of them seem so basic, he feels he would be boring his doctor if he asked them. His doctor is such a busy fellow, always in a hurry.

What is blood pressure?

Blood pressure is the pressure produced when your heart pumps blood into the arteries of the body. Your blood needs to be under pressure to move it forward so that the arteries can carry it to the organs, tissues and cells of the body (arteries carry blood away from the heart, veins generally carry blood towards the heart). As the heart beats, the pressure rises to a maximum level, called the systolic blood pressure, and as it relaxes, it falls to a minimum level called the diastolic blood pressure. When your doctor tells you that you have a blood pressure of 120 over 80 (written 120/80) it means your systolic blood pressure is 120 and your diastolic blood pressure is 80 millimetres of mercury; that is, your blood pressure is rising to a maximum of 120 millimetres of mercury as the heart beats, and falling to a minimum of 80 millimeters of mercury as the heart relaxes.

Why does the pressure not fall to zero when the heart relaxes? This is because of the elasticity of the arterial walls. Imagine you are blowing up a rubber balloon. You force air into the balloon. When you stop blowing and take your mouth away the air is forced back as the balloon deflates, because of the elastic nature of the rubber. If you close the opening with your fingers, the air remains under pressure inside. The great arteries of the body behave somewhat like the balloon. They are stretched when the heart contracts, and by 'springing back' after the heart beat, they cause the blood to remain under pressure. This residual pressure is what we call the diastolic pressure.

What is the significance of systolic and diastolic blood pressure?

Systolic blood pressure tends to be more labile than diastolic blood pressure. This means that systolic blood pressure changes quickly and goes up and down with changing circumstances. When you are exercising, or under mental stress, it is your systolic blood pressure which changes first. Changes in diastolic blood pressure occur more gradually and more evenly. Doctors have therefore assumed that a series of diastolic blood pressure readings will give a better indication of your average blood pressure, than a series of systolic readings. They have put more emphasis on diastolic blood pressure when evaluating your risk of stroke or heart disease.

Recently however, some studies have suggested systolic blood pressure is important too, and it is now generally agreed that 'systolic hypertension' (a series of readings in which systolic blood pressure is found to be raised most of the time, diastolic being normal) should be treated.

As people get older their arteries tend to harden as cholesterol, calcium and other substances get deposited in the arterial walls. The arteries no longer act in a flexible, accommodating way, but more like a steel tube. Each heart beat produces a sharp rise in pressure followed by a sharp fall as the heart relaxes. Elderly people commonly have systolic hypertension. The value of treating elderly folk with hypertension needs to be weighed against risks involved in sudden lowering of blood pressure. The general consensus at present seems to be that, at least up to the age of 80 years, high blood pressure in the elderly should be lowered, but gradually.

How does the body control blood pressure?

Supposing you wish to water the vegetable garden using a hose connected to the garden tap. You would like a jet of water to leave the hose under pressure so that it will reach a row of cabbages in the middle of the garden. There are two ways you can do this. You can either turn the tap up to full bore, or you can put your finger over the end of the hose. Both will increase the water pressure in the hose and hence increase the force by which the water is pushed out the end. Sometimes when you put your finger over the end of the hose, you find to your dismay that a jet of water appears from a hole or split in the hose further back. So there are actually three things you may do to increase the pressure, and the third is to stop any leaks from the hose.

The body constantly needs to vary the pressure of the blood to make sure that blood is forced into the vital organs at an appropriate pressure for the moment-by-moment needs of those organs. When you are lying down, very little blood pressure is needed. Yet when you stand up, the blood pressure must rise otherwise there would not be enough pressure to overcome gravity and insufficient blood would reach the brain. When you take exercise, especially strenuous exercise, the blood pressure must rise again, to allow blood to be forced into the muscles at the rate they are needing it. Therefore, there are times when everyone's blood pressure rises to quite high levels. This is normal.

How does the body vary blood pressure? Just as we found in our garden hose analogy, there are three main ways the body can increase the pressure of the blood. Either it can increase the amount of blood entering the arterial system, which it does by increasing the heart's rate and force of contraction (like turning up the tap), or it can constrict the arterioles, the medium-sized arteries around the body (like putting the finger over the hose). Or it can decrease the amount of fluid flowing out of the system via the kidneys, which is like plugging a leak in the hose. Every time you stand up, every time you move your body or take exercise, all these things happen in a beautifully monitored and co-ordinated way, without the need for any conscious input from you.

Keeping the blood pressure at appropriate levels is an exquisite example of the body's ability to maintain its internal constancy (homeostasis). In the great vessels of the body, the aorta and the carotid arteries, are tiny pressure receptors, called baroreceptors, which monitor, second by second, the pressure within the artery walls. These send messages to a part of the brain, the brain stem. There the messages are processed and result in nerve impulses being sent to the heart, telling it either to speed up or slow down, or increase or decrease its force of contraction. Other messages are also sent to the smooth muscles of arterioles telling them to contract or relax, while still others are received from and sent back to the kidneys which have a part to play in the control of blood pressure through the secretion of a hormone called renin. This is a simplified picture only. Cardiac peptides and hormones within the blood vessel wall are among numerous other checks and balances in a complex neural and hormonal interplay. The common final pathway is our blood pressure being at the right level for the moment, every minute of the day.

How do you measure blood pressure? What are you doing when you blow up that cuff?

The most direct way to measure blood pressure would be to insert a cannula into one of the great arteries and connect it to a glass tube which you would hold up vertically in the air so that the pressure of the blood would force it to rise up in the tube to the point that its own weight would allow it to rise no further. This point would then provide a measure of the systolic pressure. In fact blood pressure was first demonstrated in exactly this way, by a clergyman, Stephen Hales, who in 1733 inserted a tube into the carotid (neck) artery of a horse and found to his surprise that the blood rose nine feet in the glass column. Cannulation is still used in some scientific experiments where a very accurate or continuous measurement is required. In these cases, the brachial artery of the arm is usually selected.

In practice we use a sphygmomanometer, a much more convenient, indirect method of measuring the pressure of the blood. The invention of the sphygmomanometer is generally credited to one Scipione Riva-Rocci in Turin in 1896 and it involves the familiar routine of stopping the blood flow through the brachial artery by constricting it with a cuff. The pressure in the cuff is readily measured by noting how far it displaces a column of mercury contained in a glass tube, connected to a thin rubber hose from the cuff. The rise in the column of mercury is calibrated in millimetres, hence the blood pressure is measured as so many 'millimetres of mercury'. Mercury is used because it is so much heavier than water. If water were to be used, the column would have to be almost two metres tall to counterbalance the pressure of the blood. When your doctor inflates the cuff which she has put around your arm, the pressure inside the cuff presses on the brachial artery and, when it exceeds the pressure of the blood pushing the arterial wall outwards, the artery collapses inwards and no blood can flow through. Your doctor then steadily releases the pressure in the cuff and listens carefully with the stethoscope over the brachial artery where it passes close to the skin near the front part of your elbow. At the moment when the pressure in the cuff equals the maximum blood pressure produced by the heart, blood is able to squirt through the artery again. In doing so it makes a noise. On hearing that sound your doctor notes the pressure in the cuff. This is equal to the systolic pressure. The sounds which the blood makes as it forces past the constriction change as the cuff continues to be deflated (these are called the Korotkoff sounds) until it finally disappears. Its disappearance is commonly accepted as corresponding very closely to the diastolic, or heart-resting, blood pressure.

When taking the blood pressure the patient is usually seated with the arm at the level of the heart. Lying and standing measurements can also be taken, the latter being particularly useful in assessing the ability of the body to respond to an increased blood pressure demand. Often, on standing, the blood pressure falls in elderly patients, for example.

This procedure gives us a convenient and non-invasive method to measure your blood pressure. It is very handy when trying out methods of blood pressure treatment, since blood pressure can be measured many times without causing any harm whatsoever. This gives us a clear indication of whether a new treatment is working or not, at least as far as lowering your blood pressure is concerned.

Although convenient, the mercury sphygmomanometer is not without its difficulties. Firstly, there are uncertainties associated with the measurement itself. Since the inception of the sphygmomanometer there has been controversy about the optimum size of the cuff, the optimum length of the cuff, how the cuff should be placed on the arm and whether larger cuffs are needed for larger arms. There has also been debate about which Korotkoff sound most accurately reflects the diastolic pressure and how accurately people should try to read the 'terminal digit' (i.e. whether 84 mm Hg should be 'rounded up' to 85). Consensus has been reached on the latter two areas (disappearance of the Korotkoff sounds represents diastolic; don't 'round up' the figures, take to the nearest 2 mm Hg).

It is not at all certain, however, that in practice all doctors are following the guidelines. Other factors, such as whether the patient is sitting or lying, whether right or left arms are used, and whether the cuff is at the level of the patient's heart may all affect the blood pressure reading but may not always be recorded or carried out. These may seem like finicky details, but the measurements are being used to determine whether a person needs to submit him or herself to a lifetime of medication. Sadly, as many as 30 percent of cases of mild to moderate hypertension are thought to be misdiagnosed by observer error.[2]

Added to the sphygmo's woes is the fact that mercury is a particularly poisonous substance when ingested or when its vapours are inhaled. Sweden, Finland and France have all banned its use, not because there is any known risk in the normal use of devices like the sphygmomanometer, but because of the environmental danger from seabed and other pollution, when such instruments are discarded. Doctors may soon have to turn to the aneroid sphygmomanometer, which uses a loaded spring rather than the weight of mercury to measure the cuff pressure against. These are accurate as long as they are well maintained, but not as reliable as the mercury devices. Another alternative is the semi-automatic digital electronic sphygmo-manometer. Although more expensive, these devices can be accurate and can be purchased and used at home by the patient. You should check with your doctor which brand is recommended as some of the less expensive ones tend to be unreliable.

Measuring your blood pressure at home is a good idea for a new hypertensive and will often give a more accurate reading than the rushed visit to the doctor in which short-term anxiety might put the blood pressure up. A consensus among doctors seems to be emerging that home monitoring should be encouraged among all new hypertensives and those whose blood pressure is difficult to control with treatment. A series of measurements taken at different times of the day in the relaxed setting of your home will often give valuable information on your average blood pressure, which can be used in conjunction with the office readings. Continuous monitoring has shown quite enormous blood pressure variation minute to minute even in 'non-labile' hypertensives. Average home levels are almost always lower than doctors' office levels, the usual difference being about 10 mm Hg systolic and 5 mm Hg diastolic.

Sometimes the difference can be much larger than that. While I was a medical student, a fellow student and great friend of mine discovered to his horror that his blood pressure was markedly elevated. With mounting concern we measured his pressure many times over the next few days. Finally he consulted a tutor who confirmed the elevated pressures and referred him to a physician. After many blood tests and an X-ray of his kidneys were all reported normal he took to measuring his blood pressure himself, quietly and without fuss in the comfort of his own flat. To his surprise and relief, these measurements were completely normal. My friend was suffering from 'white coat' hypertension. The phrase refers to markedly elevated readings that are a result of the excitement of the moment such as when visiting a doctor, rather than as a reflection of underlying disease. This may seem a rather far-fetched and unusual phenomenon, but it is surprisingly common. According to one authority, up to 20 percent of people receiving antihypertensive treatment have sustained white coat hypertension and unless they have other major cardiovascular risk factors they do not need medication.[2] It is definitely worth checking to make sure you are not in this group.

Because acute psychological states undoubtedly push the blood pressure up, a common mistake is to assume that the suffix 'tension' in the word hypertension refers to anxiety or tension in the psychological sense. Hypertension can also be present in the absence of any obvious anxiety or psychological distress. 'Tension' in this context means not anxiety, but pressure. (In fact, the French say *tension artérielle du sang* for blood pressure.)

Ambulatory blood pressure measurement can be helpful in defining whether white coat hypertension is present.[3] The patient carries around, usually for 24 hours, a device which automatically inflates a cuff and takes measurements at pre-set intervals, say hourly. Such measurements are useful in studying the diurnal (daily) variation of blood pressure. They may also be used when a subject's blood pressure is borderline and the decision whether to treat is unclear, when the blood pressure is very changeable (labile), or when blood pressure is poorly controlled. Because these devices are expensive and need expert technical input in their setting up and monitoring, they are not generally used in community medical practice.

Other methods of taking the blood pressure do exist, but are mainly limited to research or specialist medical applications. For example, the pressure of the arterial pulsation in a finger can be detected using a device called the photoplethysmograph and this has found application in obstetrics and anaesthetics.

> ... all adults, young and old, whether feeling well or not, should have their blood pressure taken.

So how often should I measure my blood pressure? If I feel well, do I need to measure it at all?

Since blood pressure is such an easy and convenient measurement, and since it has been shown to be a marker or warning of underlying disease, then all adults, young and old, whether feeling well or not, should have their blood pressure taken. According to the British Hypertension Society guidelines,[4] adults should have their blood pressure measured routinely at least every five years until the age of 80 years. Those with high-normal values (135–139/85–89 mm Hg) and those who have had high readings at any time previously should have their blood pressure re-measured annually. If you are taking the oral contraceptive pill, then blood pressure should be measured at least three-monthly and if you are on antihypertensive medication, are diabetic or have kidney or hormonal disease your doctor may wish to measure three-monthly or even more frequently. Although it is not usual practice to measure children's blood pressure routinely this can be useful in the presence of, for example, kidney disease.

If I don't have high blood pressure, do I need to read this book?

Forewarned is forearmed. We are all at risk of developing high blood pressure. Even if we do not, it would be a mistake for anyone to believe him or herself immune to the risk of heart attack or stroke. The aim of this book is to tell you not only the story behind the phenomenon of blood pressure, but how you can make simple changes to your diet and daily routine that will help protect you from these number one killers in industrialised society.

How can you say what my blood pressure is when it is changing all the time?

It is true that the blood pressure changes beat by beat. During the day it is higher than when you are asleep at night and it is usually higher in the morning than the afternoon. When we take your blood pressure, we are aiming to find out your average pressure—to find out what your blood pressure is doing 'most of the time'. To do this, in theory the more measurements we take the better. Obviously it is not practicable to measure every second minute of the day for weeks on end, and a compromise has been reached that gives us a reasonable indication. Four readings over a period of four weeks is a good guide. Certainly one isolated reading is not enough. Cresswell Jones might not have hypertension, since his doctor has only one reading to go on. It is easy to see why his blood pressure might have been a little more elevated than usual the day he saw his doctor! The blood pressure should be measured at least twice at each visit and when greater accuracy is required, for example for research purposes, the average of the last two of three measurements should be recorded (the first measurement is almost invariably higher than the second two since the patient usually becomes more relaxed after the first measurement).

Many people have the mistaken idea that any rise in blood pressure is likely to instantly tear their blood vessels open and cause a catastrophic stroke. They become nervous about their blood pressure and want to measure it often. In fact, short, sharp rises in blood pressure occur quite normally in all of us. It is when these rises are sustained over a long period of time that they become dangerous. This is because persistently high levels of blood pressure are associated with the development of atherosclerosis, the infiltration of fats and cholesterol into the walls of the blood vessels, that can eventually lead to blockage or weakening of the vessel. This occurs over time. Exactly why it happens is not fully clear. It has been thought that the repeated mechanical over-stretching or shearing effect on the artery may play a part, especially if there is a wide gap between systolic and diastolic pressures (although, as we shall explain in a later chapter, a more likely theory is that the vessel wall is not stretched enough). It may be that certain hormones associated with the development of high blood pressure also promote the development of atherosclerosis. In any case, while we need to ensure that blood pressure is in the normal range *most* of the time, we do not need to be so concerned about the sharp rises that occur sometimes in the course of our daily activities.

Occasionally patients become almost obsessed with their blood pressure readings. I have one patient who, in spite of my protestations, every week faxes (with a copy to his cardiologist), several pages of neatly arranged, closely typed blood pressure readings taken with meticulous care each day. A check every week or two at different times of the day is really just as useful as a raft of very similar readings.

If you have decided to measure at home, it is as well to see your doctor from time to time to discuss your readings and see how they tally with hers. There is no point in living in 'cloud cuckoo land', dreaming that you have cured yourself if you haven't.

How high is too high? How do you define high blood pressure?

When we sit an exam, make love, or take part in a 100 metre dash our blood pressure quite naturally rises. This is normal and part of the body's incredibly intelligent response to the changing demands imposed upon it. We all have high blood pressure from time to time. It is only when it is *consistently* high that we call it hypertension. So far so good, but how do we define what is normal blood pressure then, and when can we say it has become too high 'most of the time'?

> . . . optimum blood pressure is quite literally a HOT question.

Doctors decide these things by convention. This might sound rather dry and unexciting. One imagines a convocation of grey-faced doctors gathered perhaps in Stockholm or Geneva, considering the outcomes of various trials, and reporting the results of their deliberations in obscure journals to their yawning colleagues.

It is not like this at all. The British Hypertension Society (BHS)[4] and the World Health Organization (WHO)[5] among other international organisations, do publish guidelines on what they consider to be 'too high', 'normal' and 'optimal' blood pressure. I do not know whether their committee members have grey faces, but I do know that their reports generate very strong feelings indeed.

What is optimum blood pressure is quite literally a HOT question. Huge amounts of money hang on it. Based on the answer, doctors all over the world will make their decisions about whether or not millions of patients should be treated with expensive tablets. Obviously those who make the tablets have a huge amount to gain or lose. The defining levels for hypertension are based on interpretations of morbidity (sickness) and mortality (deaths) data. At first, back in the 1920s, this data was gleaned mainly from health insurance statistics. More recently, better data has come from surveys of large populations. The most important of these, since it is the only one that directly aimed to investigate the level of optimal target blood pressure, was carried out only very recently, the Hypertension Optimal Treatment (HOT) trial.[6]

Recently the WHO lowered its recommended optimal or 'target' blood pressure. 'Normal' blood pressure they now define as below

130/85 mm Hg and 'optimal' as below 120/80. This caused a ruction in medical circles, many doctors seeing it as a drug-company-led move to promote even more widespread use of drugs. 'Any normotensive physician could become hypertensive by reading the new guidelines for the management of mild hypertension,' thunders a professor from India. 'How is it that the leaders in the health field are subtly promoting new and . . . more expensive drugs?' Drugs are a quick fix that may be dangerous. There is no short-cut, he warns, 'from the diagnostic laboratory to the clinic, except one that passes too close to the morgue'! Other doctors are alert and moving to resist the pressures of the marketplace. In 1999, after widespread discussion among family doctors on the Internet, a total of 888 family doctors, specialists, pharmacists and scientists from 58 nations felt moved to write to the Director-General of the World Health Organization, expressing concern about the new WHO guidelines. 'We fear that the new recommendations will be used to encourage an increased use of antihypertensive drugs, at great expense, and for little benefit,' state the doctors.[7]

The HOT study cost millions of dollars. Who funded it? Why, a pharmaceutical company! These doctors express concern that the same pharmaceutical company that sponsored the HOT study 'is overly anxious to promote the new guidelines. In early February [of 1999] [the company] embarrassed WHO by announcing the new guidelines ahead of schedule at a press conference in London. [The company] has also been running advertising campaigns in medical journals . . .' These doctors are to be applauded, for they smell a rat.

As we said in our first chapter, powerful forces are at work. Such forces would like us to believe that there is a certain 'inevitability' about hypertension, with pharmacological products our only real defence against it. Certainly the average blood pressure in a Western population does inexorably rise with the age of the population. In other words, for most Westerners, blood pressure rises as we get older. Thus hypertension can be made to seem somehow 'normal' (in the sense of inevitable). There are at least five senses in which the word normal is used in medicine. In this case it is being used in the sense of conforming inevitably to a cultural norm. Is high blood pressure inevitably our lot? Well, for the Tukisenta people in the New Guinea Highlands, the Kalihari Bushmen of Southern Africa and the Yanamamo Indians of South America, the answer is definitely no. In these cultures the rise in blood pressure with age so familiar in industrialised countries simply does not occur. Hypertension and its associated scourges, cardiac disease and stroke, are almost unheard of among these people.[8]

Descriptive surveys tell us what is 'normal' blood pressure in the sense of what is usual or 'average'. This is a different use of the word 'normal'. It is worth noting that average blood pressures among natives of New Guinea and some countries in Africa run at about 110/70 throughout life. This is lower than the 'optimum' level defined by the HOT trial—and all without the help of that pharmaceutical company!

You may be normal but are you perfect?

So what is 'normal' blood pressure? In the end, while we can say that there is definitely a level above which blood pressure is dangerous, an exact definition of what is 'normal' has not been agreed upon. My own feeling is that much of the difficulty in defining 'normal' blood pressure comes from a fundamental confusion between the different senses of the word 'normal'. When patients ask me, 'What is a normal blood pressure?' I have come to realise that they are generally asking what is 'ideal', or 'perfect' blood pressure. This is the sense in which they are using the word normal and it is a perfectly legitimate sense. They want to know what is the best blood pressure, what is the blood pressure that 'God intended'. When doctors say, 'Well, normal blood pressure is around the 120 over 80 for most people' they are using the word 'normal' in a completely different sense again. They are using the word in the sense of 'not associated with too much illness'.

So we have five uses of the word normal, only two of which are commonly employed by patients. The three that are usually used in medicine are i) conforming to a cultural norm, ii) the usual, iii) not ill. The two that are usually implied when a patient uses the word are closely associated with each other and can be regarded as the same: iv) operating as intended and v) perfect, the best.

I have called this book *Perfect Blood Pressure* because I think patients and doctors need to know that they have been talking at cross purposes. 'Normal blood pressure' has different meanings for patient and doctor, and doctors are not answering the questions that patients ask. Patients are really asking how to create ideal blood pressure. How to create normal (usual) blood pressure is not actually a good enough reply. Patients know that plenty of people with normal blood pressure go on to have heart attacks and strokes, so something is wrong somewhere. A set of normal measurements does not necessarily mean you are healthy. Health implies wholeness—a lot more than a few normal measurements. So this book sets out to discover perfect blood pressure.

> I have called this book *Perfect Blood Pressure*, because I think patients and doctors need to know that they have been talking at cross purposes. 'Normal blood pressure' has different meanings for patient and doctor, and doctors are not answering the questions that patients ask.

Just what perfect blood pressure is will occupy the latter two-thirds of the book. However, in the meantime we need some practical guidelines—some figures to hang our hats on. In my view, in spite of my colleagues' concern, the WHO is probably right to aim its sights at the low end of the spectrum. If setting a low target blood pressure simply allows those with vested interests to successfully market more drugs, then that is not a good situation. Doctors are right to get upset. However, drug therapy is not the only option in achieving ideal blood pressure. This is not an either/or situation—we do not have to choose between drugs or sub-optimum blood pressure. The answer is to explore less harmful and expensive methods—steer away from drugs as much as possible, and use them only when they are necessary. I base this not only on the findings of very low average blood pressures among non-industrialised communities such as mentioned earlier, but also on the significantly lower average blood pressures amongst certain groups in our own Western populations, notably those who become vegetarian[9] and those who practise Transcendental Meditation regularly.[10] Transcendental Meditation is the cornerstone of Maharishi's Vedic Approach to Health. I will explain both Transcendental Meditation and Maharishi's Vedic Approach to Health in detail in later chapters, since the beneficial effects of this approach on blood pressure are important and have been the subject of many studies.

A recent study reported in *The Lancet* also supports the view that it is better to have a blood pressure at the lower end of normal (usual) than at the higher end. This study showed that cardiovascular deaths can be predicted by blood pressure levels recorded in adolescence and early adulthood. Researchers from the University of Bristol and University of Glasgow studied the blood pressures taken among men while they were students at the University of Glasgow between 1948 and 1968.[11] They found that while the blood pressure readings were in the normal (usual) range for most of the students while they were at university, those that had higher normal readings proved to have a higher risk of dying from coronary heart disease and stroke. So low normal is better than high normal as far as future illness is concerned.

We can see that what is considered 'normal' for some populations is not 'normal' for others. Could there be different levels of 'normal' among individual people? Is 'normal' for me 'abnormal' for you? Is 'normal' blood pressure a personal thing that varies from person to person?

Although we would probably all do well to aim for blood pressures comparable to those of non-industrialised societies, it is also probable that some people can withstand higher blood pressures than others. One person's perfect blood pressure may be different from another's. The heart and other organs (so-called target organs) such as eyes, kidneys, or brain seem to be more vulnerable in some people. For them, the process of atherosclerosis seems to occur more readily. Studies have shown that this depends on a number of risk factors. The ones we know about include your cholesterol and other lipid levels, the presence of diabetes, whether you smoke, how much exercise you get, what drugs you are taking and whether your family has a history of heart attacks or strokes.

It is accepted as good medicine these days to assess as many risk factors as possible before deciding whether your blood pressure is 'normal' or 'too high most of the time' and whether or not you need drug treatment. Similarly your 'target' blood pressure—the blood pressure you aim for if it has been found to be too high—is defined according to these risk factors. If you have diabetes, for example, then your 'target' blood pressure is much lower than if you have not. Based on the statistics, doctors have constructed absolute risk assessment charts that attempt to define your risk of developing heart disease within the next ten years, taking into account the known risk factors that you might have.[12]

So, from a practical point of view, no *single* definition has been arrived at to distinguish between 'optimal', 'normal', 'abnormal', 'treatable' and 'target' blood pressures that might apply to all of us. The cut-off points that we use are simply a matter of convention. By far the majority of the 14 percent of people in a Western population who qualify as having blood pressure that is 'too high most of the time' have what is termed 'mild to moderate' hypertension. Their systolic blood pressure is consistently in the range 140 to 159 mm Hg and diastolic blood pressure is consistently in the range 90 to 99. Mild hypertension is a grey area between normal blood pressure levels and levels which are more immediately dangerous. If you are in this grey area, then you are definitely at greater risk from heart attack, heart failure or stroke, statistically speaking. But you have time to consider your options before submitting to medication. Most authorities agree that non-pharmacological methods should be tried for the first four to six months in the presence of mild to moderate hypertension. You at least have time to finish reading this book!

Cresswell Jones is an accountant who does not like grey areas. To help Cresswell get some idea of the kinds of blood pressure figures that doctors currently consider 'normal' and 'abnormal', here is an extract from the summary points of the British Hypertension Society guidelines for hypertension management, prepared as a guide for doctors and published in 1999.[4]

Use non-pharmacologic measures in all hypertensive and borderline hypertensive people.

Initiate antihypertensive drug treatment in people with sustained systolic blood pressure greater than or equal to 160 mm Hg or sustained diastolic blood pressure greater than or equal to 100 mm Hg.

Decide on treatment in people with sustained systolic blood pressure between

140 and 159 mm Hg or sustained diastolic blood pressure between 90 and 99 mm Hg according to the presence or absence of organ damage, cardiovascular disease, diabetes or [other risk factors].

Optimal blood pressure treatment targets are systolic blood pressure less than 140 mm Hg and diastolic blood pressure less than 85 mm Hg. [Note this is higher than the equivalent WHO guideline.] The minimum acceptable level of control recommended is less than 150 mm Hg systolic and less than 90 mm Hg diastolic.

Can I tell if my blood pressure is high?

'I just knew that my blood pressure was high today so I took an extra tablet.' 'I was sure my blood pressure was OK today, so I didn't take the tablets.' These statements, so often heard in doctors' consulting rooms, usually do nothing for the doctor's own blood pressure! While it is true that acute emotional stress or a painful headache (or anything painful) can cause a short-term rise in your blood pressure, it is not true that the presence of these symptoms is necessary for blood pressure to be too high, nor does the absence of these symptoms imply that blood pressure is low. Although some people are quite certain that they know if their blood pressure is high and it could possibly be true, these symptoms are usually of the non-specific type such as light-headedness or vague headache that are hard to differentiate from background feelings that people often have.[13] The vast majority of patients with sustained hypertension appear to have no symptoms at all and would have no idea that their blood pressure was raised unless it were measured. This is why it has been called the 'silent killer'.

Very rarely the condition of malignant hypertension occurs in which the blood pressure becomes very high indeed. This may be associated with headache, but it is generally accepted that these symptoms relate to the damage that is being done to the target organs, not to the blood pressure itself.

If I bring my blood pressure down, can you be sure I will not have a stroke, or heart attack?

No. Remember that high blood pressure is a risk factor only and there are many factors that contribute to stroke, some of which we know about and some we don't. There are many unfortunate people with normal blood pressure who have had strokes or heart attacks. In fact they usually form the majority of stroke and heart attack victims.[14] With all the 'hype' about hypertension, this may seem hard to believe, but the fact is that there are many more people without hypertension than with it, and the sheer weight of their numbers accounts for their showing up more often in the group who suffer from heart attacks, heart failure and strokes. A higher blood pressure simply increases your risk of joining that group, and a lower blood pressure decreases it.

Well, can my blood pressure be too low?

Blood must be pumped around the body under pressure, otherwise it could not reach the vital organs it supplies. Logic would dictate that if blood pressure were too low, then perfusion of the tissues of the body would not take place properly.

Anyone who has ever fainted knows that there are certain acute situations (acute means sudden, rather than severe) in which blood pressure falls to a point at which the brain is not receiving enough blood for consciousness to be maintained. In the case of a simple faint in an otherwise healthy person, the blood has usually pooled in the lower extremities, perhaps because the person has been standing for some length of time, or stands up quickly after sitting, and there is insufficient blood for the heart to pump upwards to the brain.

Again, when blood pressure has been extremely high for a period of time, the cerebral circulation (the arterioles directly supplying the brain) tend to compensate for the high pressure of blood being delivered to them by a process called autoregulation. This is a protective mechanism for the brain, but it means that the brain is now 'set' locally to handle a high pressure coming to it from the heart. If that pressure is lowered too suddenly using drug therapy, the brain may not have time to 'reset' its local arterioles and brain perfusion drops, perhaps with disastrous results. There have been instances in which patients have suffered blindness or permanent neurological damage from the over-enthusiastic treatment of very high blood pressure levels.

These are situations in which blood pressure has become low acutely. What about chronically low blood pressure? Is there an 'ideal' blood pressure below which blood pressure is 'too low'? In defining 'too low' the picture is even more obscure (if that is possible) than in defining 'too high'. According to statistics, for a non-elderly population, your risk of having a stroke or heart attack just keeps going down the lower your blood pressure becomes. This extends to the lowest pressures measured in the studies. In my surgery I frequently find younger people who appear to be getting around quite happily with blood pressures of the order of 80 or 90 systolic and 40 or 50 diastolic.

Common sense tells us though, that it can't go too low, or we couldn't function. Many of my patients who have low-ish blood pressures claim to be able to feel if it has become lower than usual. They could well be right. There is a strong popular belief that chronically low blood pressure is associated with various vague symptoms such as slight dizziness or light-headedness and tiredness, and there is some evidence to support this view. Long-term low blood pressure has been associated with fatigue and low mood in some observational studies. For example, in Gothenburg 776 men sampled randomly from a group of 1016 men aged 50 were given a quality-of-life questionnaire designed to assess their well-being. Low blood pressure was significantly correlated with lower perceived energy levels, self-confidence, health, memory, appetite, and impaired well-being at home, at work and within the family.[15] It is important to keep in mind though, that studies of this sort do not prove cause and effect. Not all the men who had low blood pressure reported these symptoms.

Some workers in this area propose that there is a group of people whose ability to respond quickly to getting up from a sitting or lying position by raising their blood pressure is impaired. Blood pressure stays lower for longer than normal in these people and the brain is relatively starved of nutriments, giving syncope (fainting) or pre-syncope which is not quite fainting, but close to it, in which the patient experiences some of the symptoms, such as dizziness. They suggest that this syndrome, called 'neurally mediated hypotension', may help to explain chronic fatigue syndrome, a syndrome characterised by profound fatigue lasting at least six months, which often comes on after an acute viral infection.[16]

Just as we found when considering 'how high is too high', many factors come into play when defining blood pressure. 'How low is too low' is just as vexed a question. In a situation of uncertainty, decisions on treatment often become a matter of convention. Sometimes the conventions change, and what was '*de rigueur*' becomes 'poor form'. For example, in the space of my twenty or so years in clinical practice I have been advised by my senior colleagues that the treatment of moderate systolic hypertension in the elderly was at first unnecessary, later necessary, then for a while unnecessary and now very necessary. More than most doctors would care to admit, trends in medicine are dictated by fashion rather than sound evidence.

Medical fashions, like other fashion areas, are themselves influenced by their culture.[17] There is an old story, apparently true, about an American opera singer in Vienna who consulted an Austrian doctor for her headache. The doctor prescribed suppositories. Not having been prescribed suppositories for a headache before, she unfortunately ate one. What can be correct treatment in one country can be virtually malpractice in another. In Germany, antibiotics are seldom prescribed in the community. The widespread use of antibiotics we see elsewhere is looked at askance. You might, however, be diagnosed as having *Herzinsuffizienz*, or cardiac insufficiency, a favoured diagnosis in Germany and one not nearly so popular in other countries. Heart drugs like digoxin are prescribed in Germany in amounts six or seven times those prescribed by their French or British counterparts. Likewise, the British patient is only one-sixth as likely as an American to undergo coronary artery bypass surgery. In France, there is a strong belief in the body's inherent healing powers, so drugs tend to be prescribed in much lower doses. The 'French dose' as it is called is likely to be half that used by American colleagues. And so it goes on to include low blood pressure. In Germany, low blood pressure is big business. There it is treated with no fewer than 85 drugs, as well as with hydrotherapy and spas. In England and the United States, the attitude is much the same as in my country. Low blood pressure is not regarded as at all serious, and most textbooks of medicine treat the subject summarily, or not at all. Unless it causes fainting it is a desirable condition that entitles one to lower life insurance rates.

My own view is that there are probably some individuals for whom general energy is low and, as a result, blood pressure is low. The treatment for this is to treat the underlying problem, in this case low energy, after which the blood pressure should return to normal. Treating just one symptom or sign is unlikely to have such lasting or satisfying effects as treating the whole person. Just treating blood pressure is not likely to solve a person's health problems and this is the case whether blood pressure is too low or too high.

What caused me to get high blood pressure?

This is usually the first thought to occur to a new hypertensive patient. It is such a simple and straightforward question, yet just the kind of question that can floor the busy doctor who long ago accepted that hypertension 'just is'.

Hypertension is divided into two types: primary and secondary. I will deal with the less-common secondary hypertension first.

Secondary Hypertension

Secondary hypertension can be explained on the basis of physical pathology. Something has gone wrong that can be demonstrated (and often corrected) on the physical level. For example, many types of kidney disease such as chronic inflammation (glomerulonephritis), infection and congenital abnormalities will result in an elevated blood pressure. Sometimes one kidney will be compromised by a narrowed artery (renal artery stenosis), leading the kidney to 'ask for more blood' by secreting a hormone called renin. Renin, via other hormones, acts to raise the blood pressure, thus forcing more blood into the affected kidney. Certain endocrine diseases such as hyperthyroidism and myxoedema are associated with high blood pressure. Eating excessive amounts of licorice can be the culprit, and of course, hypertension can also result from the administration of drugs such as prednisone or the oral contraceptive (that is why women on the oral contraceptive should have their blood pressure checked regularly). A very rare tumour known as phaeochromocytoma can also be the cause of high blood pressure.

In many of these cases these causes of secondary hypertension can be corrected. For example, hyperthyroidism can be corrected by surgery, drugs or radiation to the thyroid gland. Renal artery stenosis can sometimes be surgically corrected. A phaeochromocytoma can be surgically removed.

Primary Hypertension

Only about 5 to 10 percent of new cases of hypertension are found to have a physical cause. Alas, the other 90 to 95 percent of people who have hypertension have no such readily identifiable physical cause. The great mass of hypertensive patients suffer from what is called 'primary' or 'essential' hypertension, and it is this kind of hypertension that will be addressed in this book.

Had Cresswell Jones been among the 5 to 10 percent who have secondary hypertension, then he would be well advised to take medical advice and proceed to having it medically or surgically corrected. But supposing he has essential hypertension? At first Jones might feel comforted when he hears his doctor naming his condition. Language is a powerful tool, and when doctors give names to things it implies that they understand them, that they know what they are talking about, and that they are in control.

However, words can also be used in a windy sort of way to disguise a poverty of knowledge. A doctor who says, 'If you want to know the real name of your troubles, it's essential hypertension' is a bit like the policeman who tells you about his discovery that Mr Cronshaw's real name is Smith. So what? You are not much further forward in understanding the true nature of the gentleman. A dictionary definition of the word 'primary' is 'earliest, original, not derived'. 'Essential' means very much the same thing, namely something that 'just is' in and of itself. The term essential hypertension says little more than 'it just is' hypertension!

Enormous effort has gone into trying to find the 'fundamental defect' causing essential hypertension. Doctors often talk in a sort of shorthand way as if they have found the 'cause' of hypertension, quoting biochemical or physiological abnormalities such as levels of the hormone angiotensin or degree of constriction of the arterioles (arterioles are baby arteries, further out in the branches of the arterial 'tree'). However, none of these things represent the root cause of hypertension. Properly they should be regarded as 'effector' causes. Effector causes are relatively superficial, mechanical causes such as the force of contraction of the heart or the constriction of the arterioles. Effector causes can be controlled using drugs, and since drug therapy dominates the scene, these superficial causes are often thought of as 'the cause'. The trouble is that you can always ask: What caused that? What causes the heart to beat too hard? Why are the arteries constricted? Effector causes may seem satisfying at first blush, but on examination they do not give a satisfactory explanation for the phenomenon of hypertension.

So far, no 'fundamental defect' has been found although there have been many false alarms. What seemed like a simple path to discovery has become a minefield, so complex are the interactions between the hundreds of factors that seem to be involved. Rather than seek a single cause it is now generally accepted that there are a multiplicity of contributing factors.

Someone said that if more than seven factors are involved in any phenomenon, then understanding that phenomenon ceases to be science and becomes art! When we consider that well over seven factors are thought to be involved in hypertension and that there are almost certainly many that we have not even thought of yet, then trying to tease out all the factors becomes a very complex art indeed.

We have attended to some of the questions that have been agitating the mind of Cresswell Jones. Cresswell still feels reasonably fit and well. Why is his doctor pushing the alarm button? Cresswell can't quite believe that he needs to do anything. His next question is one that would occur to most people in his situation. It is an important one, and I have devoted most of the next chapter to it.

THREE

Maybe if I Do Nothing This Will All Just Go Away

OK, I have mild to moderately high blood pressure. I feel fine. What would happen if I did nothing about it?
Maybe nothing. You might live to the grand old age of 97. Plenty of hypertensive people have. On the other hand you might have a devastating heart attack or stroke and there is a greater chance of this than if your blood pressure was normal.

Behind heart attacks and most strokes is the condition known as atherosclerosis, or 'hardening of the arteries'. *Sclerosis* means hardening, *athero* is the Greek word for gruel, or porridge, which describes the appearance of the accumulations of lipids, or fats that abnormally thicken the inner lining of the arteries. Atherosclerosis occurs in heart (coronary) arteries, brain (cerebral) arteries and kidney (renal) arteries as well as peripheral arteries such as the arteries of the legs. As the process develops, blood platelets, lipoproteins, cholesterol and pieces of cellular debris form what are known as atherosclerotic plaques. Atherosclerotic plaque is not a good thing to have. It can slowly build up until it blocks the vessel; it can tear and thus unnaturally stimulate clotting of the blood so that a clot blocks the vessel; it can weaken the side of a vessel so that the vessel ruptures (called an aneurysm) or it can break off the side of the damaged artery (called an embolism). In each case the resulting blockage or leakage of the vessel can have disastrous effects on the organ that the artery supplies. Part of that organ, be it heart, brain or kidney, becomes deprived of blood and the affected cells may die. Death of cellular tissue in this way is called infarction. A high cholesterol level in the blood has been thought to be one factor that contributes to the formation of atherosclerosis. Hypertension is another, although, as we mentioned earlier, the exact mechanism is not entirely clear.

The organs that are affected by hypertension are known as 'target organs', the chief ones being heart, brain, kidneys and eyes. The heart muscle may become thickened, and later dilated (left ventricular hypertrophy), and as well, the heart tissue is at risk of infarction (death owing to lack of blood). The brain may be affected in a general way owing to thousands of tiny blood vessels bursting in the condition known as hypertensive encephalopathy, or a major bleed or vessel blockage may occur. A doctor will look for retinal haemorrhages and exudates in the eyes. These will indicate severe generalised vessel damage. In the early stages of essential hypertension the damage is minimal or non-existent and would not be visible in this way. If the blood pressure elevation is sustained for a long period of time, then depending on what other risk factors are present, atherosclerosis may start to develop.

This is not to be taken lightly. Eddie is a 58-year-old storeman who presented to his doctor for an annual 'checkup'. His doctor noted a mildly elevated diastolic blood pressure of 130/95 and asked Eddie if he could drop back a few times, starting from next week, to have the practice nurse check his blood pressure. Eddie does not like going to see doctors or nurses and somehow he got busy and found it easy to put off his appointment. One year later, while standing at the kitchen sink, Eddie suddenly felt unsteady on his feet and very nauseous. He was admitted to the emergency ward of his local hospital where his blood pressure was found to be dangerously high. Part of the brain called the cerebellum had been affected by a blockage of one of his brain arteries. The cerebellum is responsible for coordination. Although Eddie has been able to return to work he still has trouble with his movements and is able to manage light duties only.

Eddie might have 'got away' with the increased pressure in his brain blood vessels. Hypertension is not the only factor that comes into play here. He was unlucky. We doctors don't know for sure whether you will be lucky or not, so we play it safe and recommend that you get that blood pressure down. There are a great many factors that will determine whether you will be fortunate or not, and as we have mentioned, these factors are not all understood at present. All we know is that statistically you have a greater chance of suffering such a tragedy than if you did not have high blood pressure. This is the case even though you feel perfectly well at present. It is rather like driving a car with worn-out seat-belts. You might get away with it because there are many factors involved in having an accident. But you are taking a risk.

In fact we could illustrate levels of hypertension rather like this:*

Levels of blood pressure	Rather like
Normal i.e. no higher than 135/85	Driving a well-serviced car, and wearing seat-belts. Could be injured, but less likely.
Mildly elevated, no other risk factors 135–139/85–90 + Smoking cigarettes + High cholesterol + Diabetes	Good car. Seat-belts look okay, but a little worn. May not be as safe as they look. Driving fast. Oil on the road. Speedo not working.
Moderately elevated 140–159/90–99	No seat-belts, brakes worn.
Markedly elevated 160–99/100–109	Brakes dodgy, no seat-belts. Steering a bit loose. Getting dangerous.
Grossly elevated >200/110	No brakes, no seat-belts, wobbly steering. Might still get there but getting into danger territory.
Malignant hypertension ** i.e. diastolic persistently >120	No brakes, accelerator jammed down. Disaster inevitable unless something done.

* This is a general guide for the purposes of understanding. The statistics of car accidents may not tally exactly in this way with the statistics of cerebrovascular risk.
** Malignant hypertension is explained in Chapter Four.

For years people drove their cars without seat-belts. Most of them got away with it, especially if they took the trouble to become good drivers. For years mild hypertension went unrecognised. Not everybody had strokes. A car cannot be said to be 'sick' if it lacks seat-belts in the same way it would be 'sick' if its chassis were full of rust. However, doctors think mainly in terms of 'sick' or 'not sick' and this fostered the perception among them that mildly elevated hypertension is a disease that should be treated with drugs. It is easy to understand why the medical profession reacted in this way—anything to relieve the population of three evil scourges. Strokes, heart attacks and heart failure are no joke at all and there is no room for anyone to be complacent about them.

What exactly is a stroke? How will I know if I'm having one?

A stroke occurs when part of the brain is affected by an alteration in its blood supply. In a full blown (or completed) stroke, that part of the brain that is affected, dies. In most cases this is owing to a blockage of a blood vessel leading to starvation of the brain cells (ischaemia) which need a steady supply of oxygen and glucose to survive. As mentioned above, when cells die in this way it is called an infarction. A cerebral infarction is death of brain tissue as a result of blood vessel blockage. In some cases of stroke, brain tissue dies as a result of bleeding or haemorrhage from a blood vessel. Quite commonly, when a blood vessel blocks, the alteration in blood supply is temporary and reversible. Blood clots inappropriately in areas of the artery damaged by atherosclerosis and sometimes the clot can break up and move on. That part of the brain that was supplied by the vessel then recovers and the symptoms resolve. This is called a transient ischaemic attack (TIA). By international convention, symptoms that last longer than 24 hours are considered a completed stroke and not a TIA. In certain racial groups, the Chinese, for example, haemorrhage can account for up to 25 percent of all strokes. In the European population the proportion is lower, about 15 percent.

It has not proved possible so far to determine who is going to have a stroke. However, certain factors are known to increase your chances.

Risk Factors for Stroke

The risk factors for cerebral infarction (brain blood vessel blockage) are:

- ❏ Increased age
- ❏ Increased blood pressure
- ❏ Smoking
- ❏ Diabetes
- ❏ Increased blood cholesterol
- ❏ Excessive alcohol consumption
- ❏ Angina or previous heart attack
- ❏ Previous stroke or TIA
- ❏ Irregular cardiac rhythm

In addition there are a number of rarer risk factors including damaged or artificial heart valves, arterial inflammation and some blood disorders.

The risk factors for cerebral haemorrhage (bleeding) are:

- ❏ Increased blood pressure
- ❏ Aneurysms (weaknesses in the blood vessel wall, causing swellings in the wall)
- ❏ Abnormalities in blood clotting (for example, the 'thin' blood brought about by certain drugs such as warfarin)

Symptoms of Stroke

You will have little or no warning of a stroke. The symptoms usually occur abruptly as the blood vessel blocks or bleeds. The particular symptoms depend on what part of the brain is affected. Common symptoms are:

- ❏ Weakness or paralysis (usually, but not always, on one side of the body)
- ❏ Loss of speech, ability to understand language and to read (all in varying degrees)
- ❏ Loss of part of the vision
- ❏ Double vision
- ❏ Difficulty swallowing
- ❏ Loss of balance

❑ Impaired awareness of parts of the body
❑ Confusion
❑ Feelings of numbness, pins and needles

The patient may experience loss of bladder or bowel control. Loss of consciousness may occur at the onset of the stroke, and if this persists it is a poor prognostic sign.

Treatment of Stroke

The majority of patients who have a stroke need to be admitted to hospital for assessment and treatment. Blood tests and a brain scan (either CAT scan or MRI scan) are usually performed, mainly to differentiate between the two types of stroke (blockage or bleeding types) since these are treated differently. Ultrasound scans of the heart and carotid arteries are usually also performed to attempt to find the source of blood clotting.

For haemorrhagic (bleeding) strokes, the blood pressure is controlled and drugs avoided that interfere with blood clotting. In the case of aneurysm (rupture) in which a congenital weakness has caused a vessel to burst, delicate neurosurgery may be attempted. In ischaemic (blockage) strokes, thrombolytic drugs (drugs that break up clots) may be given under certain circumstances. Obviously it is very important to be sure that the stroke is not haemorrhagic before these drugs are given.

The patient may also need hydration (fluid replacement) via an intravenous line (drip), prevention of bed sores, prevention of pneumonia and often a great deal of nursing care, depending on the extent of brain damage. While the area of brain that has died will never recover, there is a large area of brain surrounding that portion that is affected by swelling. This swelling goes down over time and the patient will frequently regain a great deal of function, especially within the first month after the stroke.

In my country, New Zealand, cerebrovascular diseases (strokes) account for 9 percent of all deaths. There has been a steady and persistent improvement in the death rate due to stroke in the last twenty-five years in most countries, for both men and women. In New Zealand, death rates have fallen by 56 percent in men and 60 percent in women between 1970 and 1996.[18] This may well be owing to the better control of blood pressure using drugs.[19] However, we should remember that the cause of stroke is multifactorial and that this improvement could also reflect an increased awareness of the dangers of cigarette smoking and the general improvement in diet that has occurred in Western countries, among many other factors.[20]

What is a Heart Attack?

Heart disease is the number one killer in Western nations. Nearly one in two Americans die of cardiovascular disease, the rate is said to be one death every 34 seconds. According to the American Heart Association, medical services, medications and lost productivity associated with cardiovascular disease costs the US $108.9 billion dollars per year.

A heart attack or myocardial infarction happens in the same way as a cerebral infarction, except that this time it is the lining of a coronary artery that is damaged and the coronary artery that gets blocked when a clot forms on the damaged part. The heart muscle supplied by that artery dies.

Risk Factors for Heart Attack

Since in both cases atherosclerosis is the culprit, as you might expect, the risk factors for heart attacks are much the same as for stroke. These are:

- ❏ Increasing age
- ❏ Increased blood pressure
- ❏ Smoking
- ❏ Increased blood cholesterol
- ❏ Diabetes
- ❏ Excessive alcohol consumption
- ❏ Angina or previous heart attack
- ❏ Obesity
- ❏ Stress

If someone in your family has had a heart attack or angina then you are also at a greater risk of having one yourself. Women are partially protected from heart attacks, probably by oestrogen, until the time of the menopause.

. . . snorers are at greater
risk . . .

These at any rate are the *known* risk factors. Obviously we do not know them all, otherwise we could, with certainty, pinpoint and treat only those people who are going to have a heart attack and leave all the others in peace. In fact our predictions from the known risk factors are notoriously inaccurate, being correct probably only about half the time. Traditionally, of those listed above, the 'big three' are hypertension, smoking and elevated blood cholesterol. Others such as high blood levels of the amino acid homocysteine and the presence of an enlarged left chamber of the heart (left ventricular hypertrophy) are well recognised. We have all seen breathless announcements in the news media that a new risk factor has been discovered. Some are tantalising but not fully understood, such as the presence of a bacterium in the artery wall,[21] and the presence of peridontal disease.[22] Others may seem surprising at first, such as the day of the week (Sundays are safer, presumably because they are less stressful)[23] and snoring[24] (snorers are at greater risk as low blood oxygen is thought to stimulate the sympathetic nervous system, thus raising blood pressure slightly).

It all seems rather bitty and fragmented. Isn't there something that could pull all these factors together, some kind of grand factor that would bring the others into line? I've noticed when I am working on my car, that unless I can get the fuel delivery system right there is no point in even starting on the electrical system. The one depends upon the other. The human body must be much more complicated than a car. Getting the blood pressure set correctly might be of no use if some of those other factors were out of tune. There might be something we could do that would make everything else easy.

It is certainly true that getting the blood pressure right is not the full story. A recent study from the Netherlands analysing data from 12,031 men in seven countries collected over 25 years, shows that even for men with an average blood pressure reading, the risk of death from coronary heart disease varies greatly (up to 300 percent) from one region of the world to the next. For men with high blood pressure in some countries, the risk of death from coronary heart disease was lower than that of men with 'normal' blood pressure in other countries![25]

As to whether there is something we can do to help pull all the other factors into line, I believe there is. Until now we have been thinking in a fragmented way, looking at each factor in isolation. There is another way of approaching the problem, and this is to think of how systems operate 'as a whole'. We will lay the groundwork for this in Chapter Eight and explore the idea in detail in Chapter Nine.

OK, well supposing I have a partial blockage of one of my coronary arteries. Will I know if my heart muscle is not getting enough blood?

Sometimes a heart attack occurs without any pain at all (the 'silent infarct'). The patient may not be aware he or she has had one. A fatal heart attack can also strike 'out of the blue' with no warning at all. When a warning does occur, chest pain is the classical sign. Sometimes the patient feels a discomfort in the chest with light-headedness, fainting, sweating, nausea or shortness of breath on physical exercise. Warning chest pain may also often appear as a heavy, dull pain across the front of the chest and sometimes travelling into the arm or jaw. If a heart attack occurs (in which some heart muscle dies), the pain can be very severe, tight, crushing or constricting, 'like an elephant sitting on my chest' or 'like being squeezed in a vice', frequently with feelings of impending doom. Heart attack pain usually lasts for several hours.

What should I do if I get this sort of severe pain?

You should seek immediate medical help and rest until help arrives. You will almost certainly need to be admitted to hospital. An electrocardiograph (ECG) and blood tests will help to confirm whether a heart attack has occurred. Depending on the seriousness of your symptoms, your doctors may decide to perform a coronary angiogram, an X-ray in which the blood vessels of the heart are outlined. It is in acute situations such as this that pharmaceutical preparations come into their own. A range of drugs may be required to stabilise the heart muscle, lower the workload of the heart, and prevent fluid building up in the lungs. If the blood flow to the heart has been compromised you may need coronary angioplasty, in which a thin hollow tube known as a catheter is inserted into the heart arteries. A balloon on the end of the catheter is then inflated which pushes against the wall of the narrowed artery and opens it out. In other cases, coronary artery bypass surgery is carried out, in which an alternative route is constructed for the blood to flow past the blocked section of artery. This is usually made from a vessel from the chest or leg. Enormous resources have been mobilised in the area of coronary medical care and one can only stand in awe of the high level of technical sophistication that has been reached, both medically and surgically. This, coupled with the dedication and professionalism of hospital medical staff, is very reassuring. However, all doctors are agreed that if at all possible, it is good to put a fence at the top of a cliff as well as an ambulance at the bottom. Hence the move to try to prevent heart attacks before they occur.

What is angina?

Your heart can be short of blood owing to a partially blocked artery, but not so short that the heart muscle dies. The pain then is similar to but less intense than a heart attack and it lasts less than twenty minutes or so at a time. This is the condition known as angina pectoris, or angina. Angina can be brought on by physical exercise such as climbing a flight of stairs or mowing the lawn. Sometimes a coronary artery contracts temporarily, or goes into spasm, causing a reduction or stoppage in blood flow. This may cause angina. Although it is not clear exactly what causes such spasm, angina can be precipitated by strong emotional stress or when a person is out walking in a cold wind, and probably spasm is occurring at that time.

Unlike a heart attack, relief from angina follows a short period of rest. If you have angina that is becoming more severe and more frequent, perhaps coming on when you are resting, then this is called unstable angina and you must see your doctor to decide on further treatment. Unstable angina should never be ignored. Spasm, while not dangerous in itself, can occur in an artery partially blocked by atherosclerosis, in which case it may precipitate a heart attack. In any event, angina is a warning that something is amiss.

You mentioned heart failure. Isn't that the same as a heart attack?

No. A heart attack, or myocardial infarction, means that some heart muscle has died owing to lack of blood. If it is only a small amount of tissue that is damaged, then the function of the heart, which is to pump blood around the body, might be relatively unimpaired. If a large amount of heart muscle is affected, or if it is the vital area of specialised heart tissue which co-ordinates the beating of the heart called the pacemaker, then the heart might not be able to pump properly. It may then go into heart failure. Heart failure is the inability of the heart to pump.

A heart attack is only one possible cause of heart failure. Heart muscle can fail because it is affected by a generalised shortage of blood (ischaemic heart disease), by a viral infection or by the excessive consumption of alcohol. The heart may also fail because it is beating too fast or in an irregular way, or because there is leakage or blockage of a heart valve, to name a few causes.

The most prominent risk factor for heart failure, independent of its effect in promoting heart attacks, is hypertension.[26, 27] It seems that the sheer hard work of maintaining your blood pressure at a high level may itself force your heart to fail. Heart failure is the third most serious effect of hypertension after heart attacks and strokes, and the most expensive in terms of medical treatment.

How will I know if my heart is failing?

As the left side of the heart fails, blood banks up in the lungs, giving rise to excess fluid in the lungs and poor gaseous exchange. Shortness of breath, especially during exertion or on lying down, and fatigue on exertion are important early signs. Cough and wheezing (cardiac asthma) may also occur. Acute pulmonary oedema is a dramatic manifestation of left heart failure in which the lungs suddenly become severely 'water-logged'. The patient may be desperately short of breath, restless, blue, have a high pulse and respiration rate and feel as if suffocating. Acute pulmonary oedema must be treated promptly.

When the right side of the heart fails (usually the right side follows the left), the blood returning to the heart from the body can't be dealt with quickly enough. The blood banks up in the veins. The patient notices increasing fatigue, and may become aware of a feeling of fullness in the neck, fullness in the abdomen and swelling of the ankles as blood backs up in the peripheral circulation causing fluid to leak into the surrounding tissues.

If treated early, the failing heart can regain its strength. Heart failure is treated by resting the patient, giving oxygen if necessary and a variety of drugs designed to increase the force of contraction of the heart, correct irregularities of heart beat and decrease the work the heart has to do by dilating the arteries and arterioles.

Are heart attacks, heart failure and strokes all that might happen?

The heart and brain are the 'target' organs most commonly affected by hypertension. Other target organs include the kidneys and the small blood vessels in the retina of the eyes. If the kidneys have already been damaged, for example, by diabetes, then high blood pressure will accelerate the rate of further damage. The routine examination of a patient with high blood pressure should include looking at the retina of the eyes, since small haemorrhages may be seen, and blood and urine tests to exclude kidney damage. The other tests that should also always be done are a chest X-ray to assess the size of the heart, and a cardiograph for the same purpose and to exclude heart damage. In some countries other tests will be done routinely, such as an echocardiograph to detect enlargement of the left heart chamber and assess the pumping ability of the heart. More specialised tests to exclude rare causes of secondary hypertension may be ordered if the symptoms and pattern of blood pressure changes lead your doctor to suspect them.

Cresswell Jones is not keen on taking drugs. He doesn't want a stroke, heart failure or a heart attack either. He hits the books. Or rather, an ageing volume entitled Every Family's Medical Guide *that has seen the Jones family through many a medical crisis. To his surprise, it seems there are things he can do. He finds these under the heading 'Non-pharmacological Treatment of Hypertension'. Hastily taking out a pen he scribbles down the main points. High blood pressure can be lowered by:*

1. *Cutting down on salt.*
2. *Getting more exercise.*
3. *Reducing excessive alcohol.*
4. *Losing weight.*
5. *Reducing stress.*

Right. Now maybe he can come to grips with this thing. With gleaming eye, and teeth a-grit, Jones sets forth, his mind resolved.

Intuitively, Cresswell Jones feels there must be some kind of root cause for his blood pressure going too high and he is determined to find it. It seems certain that two of the more important factors are one's diet and lifestyle, including how one handles stress. We mentioned earlier that vegetarians have lower blood pressures on average than meat eaters. A recent study from the University of Naples suggests that restricted saturated (animal) fat intake and supplementation of the diet with monounsaturated fat (olive oil) reduced antihypertension medication requirements by about 50 percent.[28] A large trial recently carried out in the United States, the Dietary Approaches to Stop Hypertension (DASH) trial, involved 459 people randomly assigned to either a diet that was low in fruits, vegetables and dairy products with a fat content typical of the diet in the United States, or one that was rich in fruits and vegetables with reduced saturated (animal) and total fat. The authors of the study concluded: 'A diet rich in fruits, vegetables and low-fat dairy food can substantially lower blood pressure.'[29]

The diets and lifestyles of those countries which have a low average blood pressure have a lot in common, being low in sodium, fats and animal products, and high in potassium and fibre. Their foods are mainly starches, vegetables and fruits. These people are physically active, probably less stressed and seldom obese, so diet and lifestyle provide a tantalising clue as to the cause of high blood pressure. You might expect that such promising leads would stimulate a great deal of research. Well, there has been some very good research, but putting people on diets and convincing them to change their lifestyle is, comparatively speaking, not big business.

On the other hand, drugs *are* big business. The accumulated spending over the years in developing and marketing drugs is colossal. It is not uncommon for a pharmaceutical company to spend up to $20 million on testing a new product and perhaps $80 million promoting it to doctors. By contrast, in 1983, the total budget for investigating the relationship between diet and high blood pressure was estimated to be in the region of a mere $100,000![30] Although undoubtedly more has been invested since then, it could not begin to approach the profligate spending over the years on the development and promotion of pharmaceutical products.

Since the heart and arterioles are all under the command of the sympathetic nervous system, it is logical to think that chronic overactivity of the sympathetic nervous system could be behind hypertension. The stress or suppressed anger and frustration of living in a hectic and demanding world leads to a loss of appropriate blood pressure control. This is presently the favoured causative mechanism for essential hypertension.[31]

So when Cresswell Jones asks what caused his blood pressure to go too high, in the meantime we have to give him the best of the current medical views and say: 'Well, Mr Jones, that is a very hard question to answer because there seem to be a huge number of causes. We think it could be to do with an overactive sympathetic nervous system and this is probably related to your level of stress. It might also be something in your diet, too much meat, the wrong sorts of fats and oils, or too much salt, and almost certainly your weight comes into it. Maybe your lifestyle is too sedentary. It could also be something to do with your genetic make-up. On the other hand it might be none of these or perhaps quite likely a combination of a number of them acting together!'

Cresswell Jones is not very satisfied with this answer. There has to be some reason for this thing. He wonders vaguely whether, if doctors can't find the cause, they might be looking in the wrong place, rather like the drunk who dropped a coin on the pavement, then crossed the street to look for it under the street lamp 'because there is more light there'. He continues rather grimly with his 'non-pharmacological' activities. He can't say they give him much joy. He seems to be doing better and feeling worse. Maybe he's missing the boat here. Surely being healthy means feeling better? Increasingly, Cresswell is aware of a vague sense (he would be hard pressed to put it into words) that blood pressure perhaps involves not just one or two things but the whole of him.

We will explore this idea in later chapters.

PART TWO

Magic Bullets

FOUR

The Urge to Give a Dog a Name

There are no fixtures in nature. The Universe is fluid and volatile. Permanence is but a word of degree. Our globe seen by God is a transparent law, not a mass of facts. The law dissolves the fact and holds it fluid.

—Ralph Waldo Emerson[32]

In the first chapter we identified a number of powerful forces at play, not all of which were in Cresswell Jones' best interests. We compared Jones' medical consultation to a *folie à trois*, even a *danse macabre*, in which doctor, patient and the purveyors of pills are ensnared. You may think this a little overstated. All the guy did was go to the doctor and get some tablets, after all. In this section of the book I want to take you into the dance, so that you can see just how powerful are these forces.

In this chapter, we will look at the doctor's urge to diagnose. The subtle pressure from 'best evidence' studies we will examine in Chapter Five. In Chapter Six we will explore the not-so-subtle marketing pressures employed by the pharmaceutical industry.

Earlier we made the extraordinary statement that Cresswell's doctor was under pressure to give a diagnosis, a name or label, and that this may not always be in the best interest of the patient. What does this mean? Isn't that the doctor's job?

Often labels can be helpful, sometimes they obscure. When we make up a name we may create disease when it wasn't really there. Could it be, as I suspected after meeting Brad, that we are making more of a 'thing' out of hypertension than it really deserves? How did it get such a name for itself?

'Give a dog a name . . .' In my country the expression means that a dog who has been given a bad reputation becomes a bad dog. Hypertension was given a name. By the 1970s it had become a thoroughly bad dog, indeed a feral beast to be battled with.

> Hypertension was given a name. By the 1970s it had become a thoroughly bad dog . . .

Words can be very useful tools, but we should not fall into the trap of mistaking what was a convenient categorisation for reality. The great physicist David Bohm has written at length on the dangers of ascribing reality to what really started out as handy categories of thought. As he states:

> Fragmentation is continually being brought about by the almost universal habit of taking the content of our thought for a description of the world as it is . . . Since our thought is pervaded with differences and distinctions, it follows that such a habit leads us to look on these as real divisions, so that the world is then seen and experienced as actually broken up into fragments.[33]

The term 'essential hypertension' is a good example of such fragmentation. We have given independent reality to what is really just a cluster of measurements within a distribution of measurements in a given population. Not only have we fixed the thing by naming it hypertension, we have further solidified it with the adjective 'essential'. As we saw, essential hypertension means 'it just is' hypertension.

How concrete is this fixture? Well, when we look into it, essential hypertension is the kind of thing that is only present when it is there for a long time and we are a little vague about exactly how long it has to be present before it really is there. We are not very clear about how to define or even measure its upper and lower edges. Often it turns out that it wasn't there when we thought it was, and sometimes it is there when we thought it wasn't. Sometimes essential hypertension seems to be there when certain people are around and not there when they are absent. We are not very certain about what causes it. We have given it a name that implies that it has no cause at all, but we also think it has more causes than we know what to do with. Essential hypertension seems a shadowy kind of thing in many ways, rather like the goblins that live under children's beds.

'The Universe is fluid and volatile.' Of all phenomena, blood pressure must surely reflect the fluidity and volatility of the universe— it changes from beat to beat. Yet we talk as if it has an independent reality of its own. How did we get so lost in the 'mass of facts' as to see it fixed? I think this stems from the philosophy of reductivism. Reductivism soared to popularity in the seventeenth century, and still forms the cornerstone of our scientific approach today. It is the idea that by reducing a phenomenon to its fundamental components or bits, we can understand it better. Take a watch to bits and you might be able to see how it works. By reducing matter to molecules, distances to miles, mass to pounds, land to hectares, and time to seconds, we have taken mass, length and time to pieces. Even change itself was broken into 'increments' in the differential calculus of Newton's mathematics. This has undoubtedly allowed us to make huge strides in our technological ability. But it has come at a cost. We have become lost in a universe of fragments, a universe no longer fluid, but consisting of millions of rock-like shards.

> ... blood pressure must surely reflect the fluidity and volatility of the universe—it changes from beat to beat.

With the advent of Riva-Rocci's mercury sphygmomanometer and the recognition of the Korotkoff sounds we were able to break the pressure of the blood into bits (millimetres of mercury). It then becomes easy to group those bits that are high, and put a label on them. Thus Cresswell Jones' doctor can snap his fingers and say, 'I know your diagnosis—it's hypertension!' As we mentioned earlier this is superficially satisfying to doctor and patient alike. However, by creating a disease-label out of a series of high blood pressure measurements we are in danger of creating a 'demon' that is not really there. The label gets 'locked in'.

This line of thought that makes a fixed 'disease' out of something that is inherently fluid and changing has turned out to be of doubtful advantage in the case of blood pressure that is high most of the time.[34]

The problem with labelling people as diseased is that we are then led to treat them as we do sick people, with drugs. We over-react and come in with the heavy artillery. Making a fixity out of high blood pressure, we forget that it changes. If blood pressure changes constantly, then there might be quite easy ways to change it for the better. They may not involve medicines, or even doctors. Things like playing golf, enjoying one's family, meditating and eating a healthy diet are things everyone can learn to do for themselves!

> We over-react and come in with the heavy artillery.

Almost all known diseases, no matter how poor their prognosis, have in certain instances spontaneously got better (in medical language, this is called spontaneous remission). This means that there are certain natural laws available that can induce healing in virtually any situation. If blood pressure sometimes goes down from 110 diastolic to 105, then by the same token it may well be induced to go down to 95, 90 or 80, by continuation of whatever brought it down to 105. If it happens at all, then we should find out why it does, then create that circumstance for all.

Driving your car fast does not mean your car is sick, even though it does mean that you are at greater risk of an accident. In fact no one ever died of hypertension. As a cause of death, hypertension is not an acceptable entry on a death certificate. People die of strokes, heart attacks, heart failure or chronic renal failure, but they do not die of hypertension. Hypertension would be admissible only if it were recorded as a contributing factor to heart attack, stroke, heart failure or kidney failure. Thus hypertension is a risk factor, not a disease.

Why were we beguiled into thinking of it as a disease? Around 1925, life tables compiled by insurance companies were used to determine the statistical relationship between levels of blood pressure and the incidence of death or sickness. These tables mostly relied on data taken from single blood pressure readings during stressful insurance medical examinations, and therefore they could not have been terribly accurate. However, they seemed to show a continuous rise in mortality associated with stepwise increases in blood pressure in an insured population.

Meanwhile the serious condition called malignant hypertension had been identified and a desperate search was on to find out how to treat it. Malignant hypertension is nowadays rare. Before the advent of drugs, it was not uncommon and usually fatal, because the body's control mechanisms go so completely awry that the patient's blood pressure increases explosively. It is diagnosed when diastolic blood pressure is consistently above 120 mm Hg and definite physical signs such as swelling of the optic nerve and haemorrhages in the tiny vessels of the retina are seen. The patient complains of headache, blurring of vision and may show signs of heart failure. Mentally, patients may vary from being obtunded (mentally dulled) to unconscious. Left untreated, these people die within a relatively short period of time—a young adult, apparently healthy, could succumb within hours while doctors stood helplessly by. Overall about 50 percent would be dead within six months and most of the remainder within a year.

> In desperation doctors even tried injecting patients with typhoid bacilli.

In desperation doctors even tried injecting patients with typhoid bacilli. [19] That they resorted to giving patients a feared disease in order to ameliorate another gives some idea of the agonising clinical situation they were faced with. When the first crude yet effective blood-pressure-lowering drugs appeared on the scene in the early 1950s they were hailed with intense relief. Undoubtedly these drugs saved the lives of many.

Malignant hypertension involves less than 1 percent of people who have previously been diagnosed as having essential hypertension. It is clearly defined from its physical signs and its inevitable course. If you keep pumping air into a bicycle tube something is bound to give sooner or later. This is a different situation from a tube that most of the time has a slightly higher pressure than the manufacturer's specification. The former is dangerous, the latter might not be particularly so, depending on other factors like the strength of the tube and the type of ground you cycle over. Malignant hypertension is rather like the former and essential hypertension the latter.

Nevertheless, encouraged by the success of the drugs used in malignant hypertension, and struck by the clear and smooth relationship shown by the insurance figures, in which the lower the pressure the better the outlook for morbidity and mortality, doctors naturally began to wonder whether treating successively lower levels of blood pressure might lower the death rate among their patients. They had the insurance statistics. They also turned to data that had been accumulating in a small town called Framingham.

Framingham is a very famous town in the United States. It is famous because since the 1940s, the citizens of Framingham have been regularly pricked, prodded, measured and X-rayed, to assess the long-term effects on the heart of hypertension, high cholesterol levels, and other factors. The early reviews of the Framingham data in the 1960s confirmed that the risk of death from heart attack and stroke rose steadily from the lowest to the highest levels of blood pressure. Later, trials in which patients were randomly assigned to drug or 'dummy drug' therapy seemed to demonstrate the value of pharmacological therapy in bringing blood pressure down, at least in the case of markedly raised blood pressure.

By now, high levels of blood pressure had become generally known as 'hypertension'. What had been fluid was fixed. The demon dog had a name. It is at about this point that it appears to have taken a life of its own.

In 1972 the National Heart and Blood Pressure Education Program in the United States, acting mainly on the Framingham data, launched a large-scale campaign to educate the American public about the risks of this malign entity, the new disease. Suddenly everybody had heard of hypertension. Hundreds of thousands of people who had thought they were perfectly well found themselves hurrying to their doctor to find out whether they were, in fact, sick. Many found they were. This was puzzling and alarming, considering that they felt no symptoms. Nevertheless, dutifully they took their doctors' advice and began their newly prescribed drugs, even though most early medications made them feel giddy when they stood up. Each set of guidelines issued by this very powerful American policy-making body seemed to recommend a lower level of blood pressure at which the sickness began. Little by little, point by point, the level at which a good doctor should reach for his prescription pad became lower and lower. This process, as we have seen from the HOT trial controversy, continues to this day.

A subtle shift had occurred. Drugs developed to cure people in the otherwise fatal and well-defined condition of malignant hypertension were now being used to bring thousands of more or less healthy people under the influence of the medical culture. This process is now well recognised and has been called the 'medicalisation' of hypertension. 'By 1980, the stage of professional adoption was virtually complete, and the pharmacological treatment of hypertension, even at the lowest levels of elevation, had attained the status of a "standard procedure".[35] If you had high blood pressure you were sick. According to the definitions of the time, some 20–30 percent of the population in many Western countries were now sick and required treatment! Hypertension became the new enemy, to be resisted at all costs. Let us see, in the next chapter, just how thoroughly the battle was fought.

FIVE

The Medical Arms Race

Hypertension and the Vietnam War

I have a patient named Tommy who is a Vietnam war veteran. Tommy tells me that during the war, American forces calculated the statistical probability of the foe being present in a given terrain by entering a number of factors (such as enemy sightings or concentration of armaments) into an early computer aboard a B52 bomber, 32,000 feet above the ground. Bombs were then dropped in highest numbers on the areas in which the enemy was thought most likely to be, as calculated by the computer. As a result, as well as striking the enemy a nasty blow, vast areas of paddy fields and jungle were razed and cratered, and thousands of innocent civilians killed. This was because the data fed into the computer did not necessarily accurately predict the situation on any particular point on the ground. This policy, known as 'carpet bombing', has left huge areas of Vietnamese country-side scarred and cratered.

Carpet bombing is chillingly akin to the treatment of hypertension that doctors embarked on in the 1950s and have followed to a greater or lesser degree since. We try to make clinical decisions for individual patients using population-based evidence. It is sad that even as the B52s were carpet bombing the Viet Cong, aiming their weapons by statistical inference, drugs from the 'medical armamentarium' bombarded the general population back home. Both relied on statistics, the one shooting at a foe they could not pinpoint from such a distance in space, the other at an enemy they named but could not see—a risk, a possibility they could not hope to identify in far-off distant time.

How did the figures turn out? One overview of five major trials of anti-hypertensive medication showed that in the population surveyed 310 people were saved from having a stroke and 170 were saved from having a 'cardiac event'.[36] Sounds pretty good so far? The bad news is that in order to save those people, we had to 'bomb' 23,423 people for five years to no good purpose at all!

> It is no accident that modern medicine is extraordinarily rich in military terms.

Having 'fixed' the enemy in our sights we tried to hit it with our magic bullets, our 'therapeutic armamentarium'. It is no accident that modern medicine is extraordinarily rich in military terms. We talk of the Valsalva 'manoeuvre' or the Heimlich 'manoeuvre'. We are exhorted to 'help fight heart disease' and surgeons 'battle' to save their patients' lives. A recent advertising campaign for an antibiotic showed graphic pictures of missiles streaking aggressively into the sky. Their chief competitor featured grim photos of the Mafia!

The generals in Vietnam killed hundreds of enemy soldiers but at a horrendous cost. The clinician must count the cost of obliging large numbers of people to endure the side-effects of antihypertensive drugs, or placing them on unsatisfying diets like the low-salt diet.

The side-effects of antihypertensive drugs are not rare. One Japanese study of 6289 patients found that almost half (49 percent) of patients reported at least one side-effect while taking their antihypertensive therapy.[37] The figure increased to 61 percent among those patients whose blood pressure was poorly controlled. A higher number of patients in this group intentionally failed to take all their tablets, no doubt because they so much disliked the side-effects they were experiencing. This led to poor blood pressure control, so it appears the exercise was self-defeating. In a meta-analysis study from the US comparing various antihypertensive drug regimes, the overall incidence of adverse effects ranged from 12.2 percent to 41.8 percent with up to 10 percent of the patients in the study having to discontinue their drugs as a result of side-effects.[38]

What all this means is that while we can state statistically that our gunfire lowers the incidence of cardiovascular disease, we cannot say for certain whether it will benefit a given patient sitting across our consulting room desk. Drugs, and even a low-salt diet, may do him or her some harm. What is even more sobering is that although we saved 480 people during the above trials, we did not prevent all strokes or heart problems in the treated population of 23,423 people. Sadly, 234 people still had strokes of whom 140 died, and 934 still had heart attacks of whom 470 died *in spite of taking their medication*. For all the time and trouble we have exposed our 23,423 people to, some are still getting sick and dying. We have not eliminated the problem.

Quite apart from the expense in time, trouble and potentially harmful side-effects, we must also consider the financial cost of treating our group. The antihypertensive drug classes called diuretics and beta-blockers are comparatively cheap. At about 20c per day it would cost about $1.7m to treat our group for a year with beta-blockers. However, if we wish to use the more modern ACE inhibitors at up to $1 per day, depending on dosage it could cost up to $8.5m to treat our group for a year. Supposing we need to treat each of them for the rest of their lives, say an average of 30 years, then the cost leaps to $256m. In New Zealand the drug treatment of hypertension costs our small country some $100 million each year of which, in 1998, the ACE inhibitors accounted for a staggering $53.6m!

Drug the Many to Save the Few

So here is the epidemiologists' dilemma. Epidemiologists study the statistics of large populations. They try to get a 'bird's-eye-view', as if looking down on the population from a height. Using this approach we know with a good deal of certainty how to prevent quite a number of people in our community from dying prematurely. The problem is that we have no way of knowing *which ones*. The dilemma is should we bomb everyone, knowing that while the majority will be helped, many will be harmed. This is a fundamental problem. I accept that if the above studies had been extended say to ten years the results might have been more favourable. It is also true that because of a conservative strategy in data analysis known as 'intention to treat analysis', the numbers of events avoided by treatment may have been somewhat understated. But the fundamental difficulty remains. To save the few we need to drug the many. Should we do that? Is it ethical? Can we afford it?

> To save the few we need to drug the many. Should we do that?

For a growing number of doctors and community policy-makers, the answer to these questions is 'no', especially among the general public and community-based doctors and nurses. A group of researchers at the University of East Anglia recently compared the threshold at which consultant physicians, general practitioners, nurses and the general public would personally start taking antihypertensive drugs. Members of each group were asked whether or not they would take drugs if one life would be saved for every 12, 33, 50, 100 or 250 people treated for five years. The consultants chose 100. They felt it was acceptable to 'bomb' 100 people for five years (and, to their credit, they would be prepared to be 'bombed' themselves!) if it meant saving one life. The GPs felt that only 50 should be treated, while the nurses and the general public chose 33—three times less than the consultants! The authors point out that the 1999 guidelines of the British Hypertension Society were 'written largely by professors' and 'clinicians should not assume that their patients and professional colleagues are likely to share their opinion whether treatment for hypertension is worthwhile'.[39]

Even as the excesses of drug-bombing were beginning, the strategy was being questioned. The eminent authority Sir George Pickering deplored from the outset the arbitrary dichotomisation of normal blood pressure (undiseased) and hypertension (diseased). It was not a question, he said, of being sick or not sick. What is called mild hypertension is simply the upper end of a normal distribution of blood pressures within the population. By 1985 many more doctors were beginning to feel uneasy. The medical profession had moved 'too far too quickly' in setting guidelines for the treatment of hypertension. Slowly the profession has retrenched. Guidelines for treatment of hypertension now reflect the modern understanding that some people need medication more than others. Other factors such as the presence of diabetes, obesity, smoking, increased blood lipids, the patient's age and family history of heart disease are now taken into account.

This is undoubtedly a step in the right direction. Yet old dogs die hard. The dog called hypertension has dug itself deep into the medical and popular psyche, and the pressure is still on to prescribe. We are still hitting hypertension with our magic bullets to the tune of billions of dollars per year, causing unnecessary emotional stress in patients and completely unnecessary drug side-effects. We seem to have got hooked into a very expensive habit that we cannot properly shake. The next chapter will take a close look at those bullets, and the damage they can cause.

SIX

Five Uncomfortable Facts for Pharmacologists

Dr Feldstein is feeling particularly benign today. Last night he and his wife were treated to an excellent evening at the Charlton. My goodness! They do you very well at that place. All his friends were there, of course, including one or two from his old medical class, and very convivial it was. Can't remember too much about the cardiologist's talk, but then he kept it mercifully short. All much the same these days anyway. Almost always about hypertension. Shows what a problem it must be. Just as well they're coming up with these new agents. What was the name of the one they were pushing last night? Can't remember. Best not to remember. Then you know you're not being influenced by those silver-tongued suits. Sounds pretty effective though. Thirty-five percent relative risk reduction from death due to stroke or cardiac event. Thirty-five percent! And an improved quality of life. Maybe we should all be taking the stuff. Tolerated pretty well really too—very few side-effects at all, the man said . . .

'What do you think I should do?' The misty impression that he is being addressed slowly penetrates Feldstein's reverie. Across his ample consulting desk an anxious face, that of Cresswell Jones, melds into view. 'Jones!' he exclaims. 'Nice to see you! How can I help? Er . . . How's the old complaint?' 'Well, it's not that old,' says Jones, as Feldstein, searching for a clue, hastily flicks through the disordered pages of Jones' file. 'About three months ago you told me I had high blood pressure. I've jogged, I've

starved, I've given away all the foods I like. Hasn't done a thing. Your
nurse tells me my blood pressure's exactly the same.' 'We-ll, those things
are worth a try, but they're not usually all that effective, really,' responds
Feldstein. 'But that's no problem these days. They've found ways to
control blood pressure that really do work. Here, you take these, like I
told you in the first place.' Feldstein rakes his brain and, memory happily
restored, dashes off a scrip for the new agent so generously promoted the
evening before.

Cresswell is about to embark on a pharmaceutical intervention. Does
he really understand the implications of this? We now turn to the third
party in our *folie à trois*, the pharmaceutical industry, and see how its
particular goals might impinge on the good doctor and his patient,
Cresswell Jones.

First I will review the major players in the antihypertensive drug
line-up. This will lead us to identify five facts that should be troubling
to pharmacologists (as well as to doctors). I will summarise them here
and return to them in detail. These are:

1. Drugs do not get to the root of the problem.
2. Drugs have adverse effects that can be unpredictable, trouble-
    some and even dangerous. They can interact with each other.
3. Drugs are expensive, meaning that they may not be as cost-
    effective as other methods.
4. Drugs are heavily promoted in a way that can be misleading or
    that can skew the sober judgement of those prescribing them.
5. Many people dislike taking drugs. Compliance is notoriously
    low and wastage very high.

Let us now consider the major antihypertensive agents on the
market. Remember the story of the garden hose? If the hose springs a
leak, this decreases the water pressure. Crudely speaking, this is what
a class of drugs called diuretics do to blood pressure.

Diuretics

Diuretics interfere with the normal mineral-conserving function of
the kidney. Under the action of a diuretic, the kidney is forced to lose
salt and since water follows salt, your urine output is increased. This

means less fluid in the body, which, in turn, means a lower circulating blood volume. When your blood volume is lowered, blood pressure is lowered, just as putting your gardening fork into your garden hose reduces the pressure of water in the hose.

Unfortunately though, the body's vascular system is not quite like a garden hose. Our analogy is an oversimplification. Your body is in fact a vastly complex web of intelligence, with delicately balanced homeostatic feedback loops which act to maintain constancy—a stable *milieu intérieur* in an everchanging world. So, after a few weeks the body 'gets wise' to the diuretic and adjusts the blood volume back to its original level. We go on giving diuretics because for some reason the blood pressure seems to stay down in spite of the blood volume rising again. It is thought that the reason the blood pressure stays down is that the diuretics have a secondary, dilating effect on the arterioles (small arteries). So as the blood is pumped through a larger-bore artery it loses pressure, just as you can reduce the pressure in your garden hose by taking your finger away from the end of it, or if you have one of those adjustable nozzles, screwing it round to create a larger bore.

'If a drug is not producing side-effects, then it is not doing anything.' This piece of hyperbole, was an oft-repeated aphorism of one of the professors at my medical school. Like all drugs, diuretics have side-effects. Patients can sometimes feel weak and impotence can be a problem. Diuretics can also raise the blood cholesterol, triglycerides, and possibly sugar levels, all known risk factors for heart disease and stroke. They raise uric acid levels, which gives people gout. They also leach the body of potassium. A low potassium can give rise to dangerous cardiac arrhythmias (irregular heart rhythms). So we are giving a drug to lower the chance of heart attack or stroke that itself predisposes to heart attack or stroke! Clearly this is not very satisfactory, and although, on balance, it is considered that diuretics are still of overall benefit, they are generally avoided in those patients who have established atherosclerosis.

Beta-blockers

Other antihypertensive drugs aim to bring blood pressure down by acting on the autonomic nervous system. This delicate lacework of nerves includes those that are responsible for sending messages to the heart to slow down or speed up, or to the arterioles to tighten up or relax. They contain neurotransmitters called adrenaline and noradrenaline. Neurotransmitters are like message boys that take messages from the nerve endings to other 'relay' nerves or to the muscles within the walls of the heart or the arterioles. The first drugs which attempted to control blood pressure focused not on the nerve/muscle junction, but on the 'relay stations', called ganglions, between nerves within the autonomic nervous system. These 'ganglion blockers' undoubtedly saved lives in the early days, but their tendency to produce profoundly low blood pressure when the patient stood up (postural hypotension) as well as numerous other side-effects such as extremely dry mouth and poor mobility of bladder and bowels, made them impractical for widespread use.

Drugs were also tried which prevent the release of adrenaline or adrenaline-like substances from the nerve ending at the nerve/muscle junction (sympathetic inhibiting agents). However, these were also associated with problems of postural hypotension and impotence.

The first really satisfactory drugs to lower blood pressure with a 'reasonably acceptable' level of adverse effects were the beta-blockers. The beta-blockers act by interfering with the action of adrenaline and adrenaline-like substances on the heart. The heart (which is also made of smooth muscle and is embryonically related to the blood vessels) has receptors called beta receptors which respond to adrenaline. Adrenaline speeds the heart up. The beta-blockers block this action and act to slow the heart down. When the pump slows down, the blood pressure falls. This is rather like turning your garden tap towards the position in which it is off.

The beta-blockers have been vastly popular, being cheap and effective, and are still in wide use today. Beta-blockers are also useful in angina, since they stop the heart from working so hard. They are not at all useful in angina patients with asthma, since the same beta receptors are found in the bronchioles of the lung and the last thing an asthmatic wants is an agent which causes his bronchial tubes to constrict. Similarly, the beta-blockers can cause constriction of the peripheral arterioles and patients often report cold hands and feet in winter. This is particularly serious if they suffer from Raynaud's disease in which the arterioles are already prone to spasm, or atherosclerosis of the arteries of the leg, in which case blood supply can be severely compromised. Beta-blockers can sometimes make people feel very tired, and this is an effect which tends to creep up on people insidiously. Beta-blockers can also interfere with fat and sugar metabolism. A recent study shows that those on beta-blockers are at 28 percent greater risk of developing diabetes than controls.[40] Other side-effects of beta-blockers include insomnia, nightmares and impotence.

In the great majority of car accidents, wearing a seat-belt will minimise serious injury. In just a few accidents it might be better to be thrown clear, in which case the seat-belt makes things worse. Diuretics and beta-blockers are a little like seat-belts. They do have some actions that increase your chance of stroke or heart attack, but in more cases than not their antihypertensive effect overrides these effects and decreases that chance. When you are taking these drugs you are hoping, indeed gambling, that you are in the category of person that will be benefited not disadvantaged. You have no way of knowing which category you fit into.

Two other main classes of antihypertensive drugs have emerged in the last twenty years: the angiotensin-converting enzyme (ACE) inhibitors and the calcium channel blockers.

ACE Inhibitors

The ACE inhibitors interfere with the action of an enzyme, ACE or angiotensin-converting enzyme. Angiotensin I is a substance derived from renin, which is produced by the kidney. Angiotensin I is then converted into angiotensin II, which acts directly on the muscles of the arterioles to squeeze the arterioles tighter and hence raise blood pressure. By inhibiting the enzyme that converts angiotensin I to angiotensin II, the ACE inhibitors dilate the blood vessels and lower blood pressure.

ACE inhibitors work in approximately 40 to 50 percent of patients,[19] which is considered good in antihypertensive pharmacology circles. They are more effective when combined with diuretics or beta-blockers. Although they have the fewest side-effects of all the anti-hypertensive substances, they are by far the most expensive. Many patients will notice no side-effects at all, although in my practice I have had several patients who have developed a very troublesome cough (this is a well-recognised adverse effect). Rashes, sometimes severe, can occur as can loss of taste with one ACE inhibitor, low white blood cell count and worsening of renal function if kidneys are already damaged. If I found myself forced to take antihypertensive medication I would probably go for an ACE inhibitor, or perhaps one of the new generation of related drugs, the angiotensin II inhibitors, that do not cause a cough. There is no evidence though that either the ACE inhibitors or the calcium channel blockers would have any effect in preventing me from having a stroke or heart attack. This is because the studies that might prove this simply have not been done yet. It is one thing to show that a drug can lower blood pressure. It is another thing altogether to show that lowering blood pressure in this way will decrease the chances of a stroke. High blood pressure is called a surrogate end-point. We *assume* that lowering blood pressure will lower the incidence of stroke or heart attack, but this is an assumption only. Some argue that, rather than stroke or heart attack, total mortality (death from any cause) should be the end-point. What is the use of a drug if it decreases your chance of stroke or heart attack, but makes you feel so miserable that you commit suicide, or so aggressive that you have a car accident and get killed? There has been a suggestion that lowering cholesterol levels too enthusiastically may not be in a patient's best interests. One review found that men whose cholesterol levels were below 4.14 mmol/l exhibited 20 percent more cancer deaths, 35 percent more deaths from injury, 40 percent more non-cardiovascular, non-cancer deaths and 50 percent more deaths from digestive system disease.[41]

Maybe you won't feel that miserable or aggressive, but just a bit off-colour or mildly depressed. This has led some workers to investigate the 'quality of life' that a patient can expect on a drug regime. Questionnaires are generally used and the results are sometimes expressed with the term 'quality adjusted life years' (QALYs), which is intended to define how many extra 'good' years you can expect from a drug. There are many problems with these studies. 'Quality of life' is a vague thing to try to define. Often people will report ill-effects or good effects from placebo (dummy) pills, so it is hard to know exactly what effect a drug is having. Nevertheless pharmaceutical companies have been quick to jump on the bandwagon, presenting studies showing that their particular chemical improves the patient's 'quality of life'. QALY studies are 'a major new field as far as the marketing of antihypertensive drugs is concerned'.[13] Except that it might raise your blood pressure, you should take these studies with a pinch of salt!

Calcium Channel Blockers

These expensive drugs caused a commotion in 1995 when medical scientists published findings suggesting that the risk of having a heart attack actually rose by 60 percent in patients taking (the short-acting) calcium channel blockers. Other groups suggested that the risk of suicide[42] and the risk of gastro-intestinal haemorrhage[43] also increased among those taking these drugs.

This could be compared to a seat-belt that sometimes throttles the wearer, causing death instead of preventing it. At the time of writing, no definite conclusion on this issue has been made by the profession as a whole. Most doctors, though, avoid using the shorter-acting calcium channel blockers unless there is no alternative. The longer-acting ones can be useful, the most common side-effects being flushes, headaches, palpitations, weakness and troublesome leg swelling.

Apart from their side-effects, another problem drugs have is that they can interact with each other. One calcium channel blocker, intro-duced with great fanfare to the market, was recently abruptly withdrawn. This was because it was found to interfere with an enzyme that metabolises many other drugs, leading to the possibility that those drugs could become toxic at normal doses.[44]

There are other classes of antihypertensive drugs, less frequently used, including those that act centrally on the brain, such as alpha-methyldopa, clonidine and reserpine, about which we do not have space to go into detail here. Nevertheless we are starting to come across some of the uncomfortable facts that surround the use of drugs. Let us examine them:

Uncomfortable Fact 1. Drugs Do Not Get to the Root of the Problem

The other day a sample 'Patient Information' pamphlet fell out of my copy of the *New Zealand Medical Journal*. Made possible by the generosity of four pharmaceutical companies, it states: *Blood pressure goes up as a normal response to stress and physical activity. However, a person with hypertension has a high blood pressure even at rest.* So far so good, but then the writer continues with a brief but comprehensive treatise on the different drug therapies that are available on the market. The reader, perhaps an unhappy, worried patient, looks in vain for 'non-pharmacological interventions'. Nowhere does the pamphlet talk about even the possibility of preventing the blood pressure rising in the first place, or reducing it by natural means if it does rise. It is almost as if the writer wanted the patient to have hypertension so there would be a market for drug therapy—rather like touting a windscreen cleaner for a car without mudguards without mentioning the possibility of mudguards.

This pamphlet, designed as a patient's first port of call on learning that he or she had hypertension, illustrates the medical obsession with only the most superficial of causes of high blood pressure. The entire pamphlet mentions only those things that move and act upon each other: the heart, the blood and the smooth muscle of the walls of the arterioles. While a constricted blood vessel might be said to have 'caused' blood pressure to go too high, it is an effector cause only. It could never be the root of the problem since the question can always be asked, 'What caused the vessel to constrict?' In spite of the pharmaceutical industry's attempts to blur the issue with claims that their drugs improve the patient's 'quality of life', the hard truth is that drug therapy does nothing to address the underlying cause of hypertension. Drugs control blood pressure. They may save you from a stroke, or they may not; all we know is that your chances are better. You may still have that stroke, because whatever other factors were causing your blood pressure to go too high, those factors still remain.

Sometimes people feel 'safer' when they opt for an antihypertensive drug. Somehow pharmaceutical technology seems 'more reliable' and we can get the idea that such technology is infallible. Are drugs always effective in controlling blood pressure? Do they always work? No, not always. In fact an antihypertensive agent is doing well if it brings blood pressure down in 60 percent of cases. You might fall into the 40 percent for whom it does not work. In practice doctors try one, and if it doesn't work then they add or try another. In spite of a doctor's best efforts in this way, occasionally blood pressure remains poorly controlled. Doctors simply run out of drugs to try.

In my practice I have had a number of patients whose blood pressure has not been well controlled with drugs, who responded to the more fundamentally healing interventions of Maharishi's Vedic Approach to Health. Hilda is a 79-year-old retired nurse who at the early age of 49 had had a devastating stroke. In her case this was caused by a relatively rare congenital weakness, known as a berry aneurysm, of the arteries supplying the brain. On the evening of her stroke, she had been attending a meeting to discuss whether young mothers should be allowed to stay in hospital with their sick children. The subject was controversial and the meeting was heated. Hilda became aware of a sudden headache and began to feel very unwell indeed. No doubt her blood pressure had risen, and the artery had burst at its weakest point. Amazingly she somehow managed to drive home. Once home she vomited violently and was rushed to hospital where a delicate operation was performed to repair the damaged artery. In spite of antihypertensive drugs her blood pressure remained obstinately high. Not only had Hilda to live with the shadow of another episode hanging over her, but she had to put up with her doctor accusing her sternly of not taking her tablets! When I first met her, her typical blood pressure was around 200/100. Hilda learned Transcendental Meditation. With regular practise and a small dose of a herbal preparation, her blood pressure is now consistently in the range 160–180/76–86, a far safer level.

Uncomfortable Fact 2. Drugs Have Adverse Effects

In looking at a few classes of the most commonly prescribed antihypertensives we listed some of their adverse effects. Do these represent a complete list? Can we ever have an exhaustive list of all possible side-effects?

I recall, as a fourth-year medical student, listening to a lecturer telling us about a newly qualified doctor colleague of his working in a large base hospital. She had just learned that she was pregnant. The pregnancy was unwanted, and feeling depressed and anxious about it, she ratted through her medical bag and found a free sample of a product which a drug firm representative had left with her a few days earlier. The drug was a mild tranquilliser and she took two tablets. She felt much better and slept well that night, little knowing that these tiny innocent-looking pills were to deliver her into a nightmare that was to oppress her for the rest of her life. For later, she gave birth to a deformed child. The drug, of course, was thalidomide.

We all remember thalidomide. Everyone has seen photographs of victims of a drug marketed assiduously, then swiftly removed from the market when its effects on the fetus in the first trimester were known. Fewer people would be aware of practolol, a drug once used in the treatment of hypertension.

The Practolol Disaster
In 1970, practolol was an exciting new addition to the progressive doctor's tool-kit, the second of the beta-blockers to come on to the

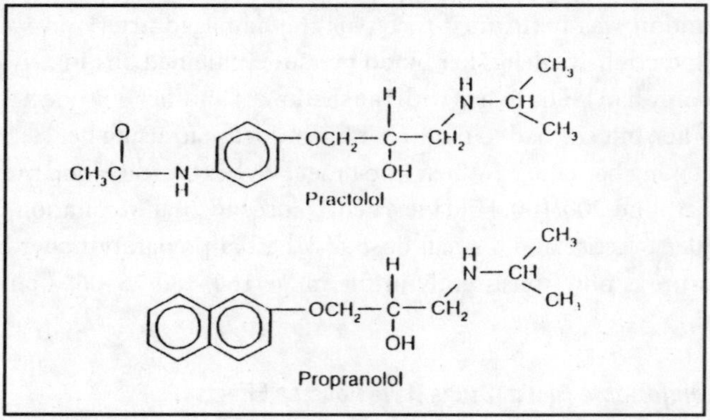

Figure 1: Spot the Villain

Practolol and propranolol molecules. The behaviour of a drug cannot be predicted by knowing about its molecules. The chemical structure of the antihypertensive drugs propranolol and practolol are almost identical. Propranolol has a good safety record, yet practolol caused a world-wide medical disaster.

market. The first beta-blocker, propranolol, had been a breakthrough in the treatment of hypertension. Like the first antibiotic, penicillin, propranolol is still used today, and is among the safest and cheapest of all drugs after years of use by millions of people around the world.

In those early days, practolol looked as if it would be even more useful. Its chemical structure is almost identical to propranolol, the only difference being that practolol has a single side chain of molecules in a position at which propranolol has a benzene ring (see Figure 1). It is an excellent antihypertensive and seemed to have some advantages over propranolol as well. But even as the pharmaceutical representatives were taking to the roads, glossy brochures in hand, something was going terribly wrong. People taking practolol started complaining to their doctors about burning and grittiness of the eyes. Since patients commonly report these symptoms, a more sinister cause than the usual allergies or viruses was not initially suspected. Others reported severe rashes, some earache, deafness and/or chest symptoms. The range of symptoms was wide and became known as the 'oculo-mucocutaneous syndrome'.[45] The membranes of the abdomen were also affected. In New Zealand, a woman complaining of dry eyes, abdominal fullness and fluid bowel motions was admitted to a surgical ward. Unable to make a diagnosis, the surgeon opened her abdomen, finding a sight of which 'she had never seen the like before in her long and extensive surgical experience. It was as if the abdominal viscera [organs] were cocooned in opaque pinkish plastic material . . .'[46] With good detective work the authorities quickly traced the cause of these new and worrying phenomena to practolol. The drug was removed from the market, but not before hundreds of people had been affected, at least three victims had become blind and over 50 had contracted 'practolol peritonitis', many of whom died an agonising death. In New Zealand, and probably in other countries, there was no register of how many people had been exposed to practolol, so the full extent of the damage will never be known.

I am sure many of my colleagues would be quick to counter these accounts of some of medicine's darkest days by citing those people whose lives had been saved from stroke, heart disease and early death by the widespread use of practolol. But should the treatment of high blood pressure be a balancing of disasters against triumphs? Is it necessary, or even right to take such risks? A patient dying of a drug-induced disorder would not feel very happy about being sacrificed for the sake of the few people who were benefited.

There is no possible scientific study that could have predicted this disaster in advance.

A drug can never be pronounced fully 'safe'. One million patient years of cumulative experience with practolol had to elapse before the oculomucocutaneous syndrome was recognised. Practolol peritonitis sometimes showed up months after the drug had been withdrawn. There is no possible scientific study that could have predicted this disaster in advance.

When Is a Drug Safe?

In the end all drugs have to be 'field trialled', with the general population (that's you and me) acting as guinea pigs. To pronounce a drug completely safe is a bit like saying that a certain airline is completely safe. A fallacious inductive logic tempts us to believe that because an airline or type of aeroplane has had an accident-free record for thirty years, it is 'safe'. Unfortunately, this is not necessarily true, as the world has seen many times over, for example, in the disastrous demise of the Concorde.

Drugs are not predictable in their effects. Minoxidil is a drug that seems to be useful for stimulating hair growth. According to an advertisement in my local newspaper, minoxidil has a low incidence of side-effects. The advertisement does not mention that minoxidil actually started out as a would-be antihypertensive agent. Researchers found minoxidil was a good antihypertensive, but it did also have this curious property that bald men's hair began to grow . . .

This means that it was doing entirely unforeseen things in organ systems that the researchers would never have dreamed would be affected. Do you find this disturbing? How much do we really know of the complex actions of drugs on the vastly intricate web which makes up the human body? We give a drug for blood pressure, and people's hair starts growing! A new side chain on a seemingly innocent molecule leaves some people untouched and causes devastation in others. How much do we know about the unique differences between us, that the drug which can be so safe in the majority is so catastrophic for the unfortunate few?

In the end, health care authorities go by statistics. Remember their goals are to do with populations, rather than individuals. Authorities promote the use of antihypertensives because, statistically, anti-hypertensives save more lives than they end. We treat our children with antibiotics and accept the occasional drug-related death (yes, they do occur) because antibiotics do save lives most of the time. It is cold comfort, of course, for the family of an innocent victim, say a child who is treated for an ear infection with a commonly used antibiotic like co-trimoxazole, then develops the rare but often fatal Stevens-Johnson syndrome.

From the authority's point of view it makes good sense to run the risk, *because there is no perceived alternative*. Drug-bombing is seen as the only way to deal with the epidemiologists' dilemma. However, there are alternatives. They do require a different mind-set, a different way of looking at things, but they exist. We will find our way out of the dilemma in a later section of the book.

Tailpiece: And in case you thought everything was under control, let me tell you that thalidomide is still being used and deformed babies are still being born. According to an article from the *Observer*: 'The world thought it had overcome the horrors of thalidomide when the drug was banned worldwide in 1962. But in Brazil, which received approval to produce the pill in 1965 to fight leprosy, the horror story has continued . . . The Movement for Reintegration of Leprosy Patients found 47 people under 20 who had been deformed by thalidomide. It also found that 10 other thalidomide babies had died shortly after birth, and eight women had aborted fetuses after sonograms revealed thalidomide-related deformities . . . Unaware that worldwide the pill deformed about 12,000 babies during the 50s and 60s, the lepers pass on thalidomide to neighbours as a remedy for colds, fevers, skin rashes, stomach aches and morning sickness . . .'[47]

Uncomfortable Fact 3: Drugs Are Expensive—Meaning that They May Not Be as Cost-effective as Other Methods

In New Zealand our tiny population of 3.5 million people consumes some $700 million worth of drugs per year. Antihypertensive medication costs the country around $120 million per year. You could run a lot of schools with that sum of money! The per capita figures for other industrialised countries are likely to be roughly the same. It might just be worth spending these sums if these drugs were cost-effective, but as we will see, other methods do exist that are just as effective and considerably cheaper and safer. The sums spent on drugs are sobering enough, but what is even more disheartening is that a good proportion of this money is completely wasted as the tablets and capsules never reach the patients' mouths. The patients either don't tolerate them, or simply do not like taking them. The fact that drugs are unpopular with their consumers is *Uncomfortable Fact 5*. But first let us look at how such an unpopular product can survive in the market.

Uncomfortable Fact 4: Drugs Are Heavily Promoted in a Way that Can Be Misleading

At a recent medical education meeting, our group of general practitioners (in my town most GPs belong to a practice organisation) was told that we were to have a 'role play'. A member of our managerial staff was to enact a visit to a GP by a pharmaceutical representative. She was to be the rep and she would introduce a GP to the benefits of a drug newly released on the market. One of our group was to be the GP.

The door opened and in stepped an attractive, well-presented woman of about 35, balancing on one hand a tray full of delectable cakes and sweetmeats. In the other hand she held strings atttached to three white helium-filled balloons which bobbed about gaily, each carrying the name of her product. On her face she wore a beaming smile. She introduced herself warmly, presented her card which revealed her as a science graduate, offered cakes all round and began asking the GP friendly and interested questions. What sort of a morning had he had? Had the practice been busy? How was his holiday? Did the whole family go? Oh, nice! How many children in your family? Does your wife work?

Her questions then switched smoothly to clinical matters. Did he see many rheumatoid patients these days? Any problems with drug-induced gastritis? He has? Quite a problem isn't it? The GP nodded and said, 'Yes.'

As she showed the GP graphs and statistics and related a story about a specialist doctor at the hospital who now uses her company's product exclusively, I began to wonder about this manager-cum-actor. Her delivery seemed too expert for even a skilled actor to mimic. At the end of the interview I asked her if she had ever done sales work professionally. Yes, she smiled, she had been a pharmaceutical representative for ten years before accepting a managerial position with our group.

We were then asked to comment on her performance. Almost all present (there were about ten of us) said that she seemed pleasant and her spiel was informative. They were soon to learn that she was not being as innocently educational as she seemed. In fact she knew exactly where she was at each point of the interview in a carefully thought-out game-plan. Her attractive dress, the balloons, the cakes, the smile, the friendly questions were contrived to attract attention and establish rapport. Details about the doctor's family, prescribing habits and reactions would later be meticulously entered into a database that could be accessed by other members of her firm. This data would be classified and graded one to five under headings such as 'positivity' or 'friendliness'. The fished-for 'yes' answer was set up to encourage later 'yes' answers. The statistics were presented in a biased manner and the appeal to a medical authority was deliberate and planned, among many other 'tricks of the trade'. Like Dr Feldstein, my colleagues had believed that they were being brought up to date on latest medical knowledge. They were, in fact, on the receiving end of a professional marketing exercise that teetered on the verge of deception.

There is nothing inherently wrong with promotion *per se*. Every time you brush your hair in the morning you are preparing to promote yourself to the world. Pharmaceutical company representatives are professional promoters, they are salespeople. It could be said that they cannot be blamed for using skills common to the world of selling. What is alarming, however, is that powerful sales techniques are being used to promote medicines that have considerable potential for harm.

In an area that is vital for human well-being, where sober and unbiased judgement is paramount, it is alarming that the dissemination of potentially harmful substances and the decisions about their use should be driven principally by those who stand to profit from their sales. This is not in the best interests of the patient. It is also of concern that the majority of medical people are untrained to recognise promotional techniques, nor do they realise how powerful and effective they are. The line between promotion and manipulation can easily become blurred. For example, it is a known facet of human behaviour that people like to appear consistent. Thus:

Doctor, do you believe that hypertension is harmful to the individual? 'Yes.'

Do you think that hypertension should be treated? 'Yes.'

Do you use ACE inhibitors at all? 'Yes.'

Based on the evidence you have seen today, do you feel now that you will use our super new improved all-powerful ACE inhibitors? . . .!

The doctor feels pressure now, not to be seen as inconsistent with his stated position. He is very likely to say, 'Er, yes.'

The 'Drummer' of the Drug House

Do these and other techniques work? They certainly do, otherwise the representatives would be taken off the road. There is a large body of published evidence that 'detailing' a drug influences its rate of prescription (detailing means one-on-one promoting). Here are some examples:

When the minor tranquilliser temazepam first came on the market in Australia, a study showed the pharmaceutical representative to be the most influential source of information for medical practitioners in both product awareness and product use. Doctors who had received visits from reps were more likely to have prescribed it and more likely to have prescribed it at an earlier date.[48]

A study in the United States looked at the knowledge and beliefs of 85 doctors with respect to a widely used analgesic and a group of drugs known as cerebral vasodilators. Sixty-eight percent believed that drug advertisements made little impression on their prescribing habits, and 62 percent believed they made their prescribing decisions based on academic sources (such as peer-reviewed medical journals). Yet when tested on their knowledge of the drugs, up to 71 percent of the doctors entertained beliefs, promoted by the manufacturers of the drugs, that were opposite to those indicated in the clinical literature at the time.[49]

In the United States in 1995, 14.4 million prescriptions for a new class of antibiotics called fluoroquinolones were filled at pharmacies. Medically speaking, there are very few situations in which they should be the first drug chosen for an infection—it is better medical practice to keep them in reserve in case a new and resistant bacterium ('super-bug') should appear. It appears that the manufacturers' efforts to promote them as drugs of first choice were effective.[50]

> ... up to 71 percent of the doctors entertained beliefs, promoted by the manufacturers of the drugs, that were opposite to those indicated in the clinical literature at the time.

Is the evidence presented by the representatives sometimes biased? In a study involving sixteen representatives and their interactions with six GPs, researchers found that instances in which reps failed to mention or minimised important risks associated with the drugs were commonplace. These risks included precautions that should be taken, warnings, adverse reactions, drug interactions and use in pregnancy. Only five out of 33 interactions mentioned information pertaining to four or more of these important categories.[51] In a study at a large university in California, a pharmacist sat in on thirteen successive lunchtime promotional presentations of drugs by pharmaceutical representatives, taping the presentation. Twelve of 106 statements about drugs were inaccurate; all twelve statements were favourable to the drug. One of the drugs presented was removed from the market twenty days after the meeting because it caused deaths. Two of the inaccurate statements could have been dangerous if they had been accepted at face value.[52]

Fudging the Figures

Sometimes statistics can be presented in a way that is not incorrect, but could give a misleading impression. Studies such as the Hypertension

Detection and Follow-up Program (HDFP) show that treatment of mild hypertension in a population does lower the incidence of strokes by 20 percent. This is what is known as the 'relative risk reduction'— the reduction in stroke-related deaths relative to the number that were occurring before treatment. This is useful, even impressive, information, but, as we saw in the section on carpet bombing (Chapter Five), for the full story it is necessary to know how many people need to be treated to create this effect. Although a 20 percent reduction in strokes sounds good, we are actually talking about changes in relatively small numbers here, because the incidence of stroke in the population of mild hypertensives is small anyway. The HDFP study showed that out of say, 1000 people treated with antihypertensive drugs, 77 would have died if untreated (as demonstrated by the control group), 64 would have died in spite of treatment, leaving 13 who were benefited and 987 who were not benefited at all by taking the medication. Even though it is not untrue to say 'deaths fell by 20 percent', what is known as the 'absolute risk reduction' was actually only 13 out of a thousand or 1.3 percent.[53] It is easy to see why drug reps might emphasise relative risk reduction and avoid talking about absolute risk reduction, because quoting the relative risk takes the attention away from the carpet bombing that has been going on.[54]

Drug studies dominate the medical literature on hypertension. Many are funded by the companies that produce the drug. A study showing that their drug brings high blood pressure down is good news for the firm, and could mean millions of dollars in profit. However, when a study does not turn out the way the company would like it to, conflict can arise. One professor of public health sciences in the US has been quoted as saying: 'Companies can play hardball, and many investigators can't play hardball back. You send the paper to the company for comments, and that's the danger. Can you handle the changes the company wants? Will you give in a little, a little more, then capitulate? It's tricky for those who need money for more studies.'[55] From the company's side, money is no object. A cardiologist friend of mine was recently flown from New Zealand to a first-class hotel in Geneva (about 12,000 miles from his home) to join cardiologists from around the world. The purpose of this meeting of learned associates?

To spend one day making sure they were all using the sphygmomano-meter in a standardised way, so that they could take part in a clincial study! Drug companies are heavily involved in medical education generally. Once doctors and patients get the message that this medication is for life then the company has a guaranteed market.

Of course there is really no such thing as a free lunch and we should perhaps not be too surprised to find that researchers who are in the pay of a pharmaceutical company are likely to cite results that are favourable to the 'company line'. One study showed that 'Authors [of medical articles] who supported the use of calcium-channel antagonists were significantly more likely than neutral or critical authors to have financial relationships with manufacturers of calcium-channel antagonists (96 percent, versus 60 percent and 37 percent respectively).[56] Funding a study seems to be good advertising, as far as a drug company is concerned.

The first pharmaceutical sales representative appeared in 1850. Soon after, Sir William Osler called attention to this 'dangerous enemy to the mental virility of the general practitioner—the "drummer" of the drug house'. Nowadays most GPs see drug reps at least once per week and sometimes three or four times. For many it is their only channel for keeping up with medical developments.

Uncomfortable Fact 5. Many People Dislike Taking Drugs

Literally truckloads of antihypertensive drugs are prescribed every year in most industrialised countries of the world. It is only comparatively recently that people have thought to ask: What actually happens to these drugs? How many go down the throats of the patients? To everyone's dismay the answer seems to be 'not many'.

A few years ago, I engaged Mike, a newly qualified doctor, as a locum in my practice for a few weeks so that I could take my family on holiday. At the end of the holiday he stayed on for a few sessions so that I could catch up with some paperwork. Working away in the next room to his, I was surprised to hear raised voices. A heated interchange was going on between Mike and one of my regular patients, a middle-aged woman who had decided that she 'felt OK now' and did not need her blood pressure tablets after all. In fact, on her own determination, she had not taken them for the last six weeks. 'Mrs Smith, you *must* take your pills. These pills will help you. It is very important to take them for the rest of your life!'

Some 23,423 people had to be treated for five years to save 480 people from having a stroke or heart attack. How do you get 23,423 people to take a potentially poisonous substance two, maybe three times per day for five years, when the chance of it doing them some good personally is actually quite low? The answer is 'with difficulty'. Many people feel intuitively that there is something deeply wrong about it. They view the idea with unease. I could not help reflecting that my evangelical locum was fighting a losing battle.

What was the chance of Mrs Smith falling in with his wishes? For how long would she persevere? How many people for whom long-term medication is prescribed, actually take it in the intended doses?

Probably about half. According to a report from the Royal Pharmaceutical Society of Great Britain, 'A search of the international research literature suggests that some 50 percent of patients who suffer from chronic diseases do not take their medication in fully therapeutic doses.' [57]

In fact only 10–15 percent of patients take 90–105 percent of the medications prescribed. (105 percent because there are some people who take more than prescribed!) As many as 30–50 percent of patients fail to achieve the desired therapeutic effect of their drugs. Fully 10–15 percent of patients do not even bother to have the drugs dispensed at the chemist!

These are miserable figures. What do they say about the value of drug therapy? Doctors have traditionally labelled this 'the problem of compliance'. People who do not take their medicine are 'non-compliant'. This terminology harks from a time when medicine was able to view the populace from a privileged position of paternal authority. Doctors knew best. People that don't follow their doctors' orders do so out of ignorance, forgetfulness, disorganisation or contrariness. They should be strongly encouraged to do what they are told. Researchers have identified many reasons that people do not take their medicines. Certainly a lack of understanding of the reasons for taking the drug and forgetfulness do play a part. However, again according to the Royal Pharmaceutical Society report: '. . . the most salient and prevalent influences on medicine taking are the beliefs that people hold about their medication and about medicines in general . . . they are firmly rooted in the personal and family and cultural experiences of us all. For the prescriber simply to reaffirm the views of medical science, and to dismiss or ignore these beliefs, is to fail to prescribe effectively.' What this means, as I read it, is that people don't feel good about taking drugs and doctors should not try to force the issue.

'Non-compliance' is, then, a kind of spontaneous civil disobedience. In my town we now have a 'compliance committee'. 'Non-compliance is *the* major problem in therapeutics', according to their recent report. They estimated the wastage to New Zealand with its tiny population of 3.5 million people is of the order of $200–350 million per annum. $350 million every year! Assuming that a million dollars worth of medicines might fill a removal van, that's 350 vanloads of pills simply being left to go out of date in cupboards and medicine cabinets, being dumped in rubbish bags or flushed down toilets. The wastage on the global scale must be astronomical!

> 'Non-compliance' is . . . a kind of spontaneous civil disobedience. In my town we now have a 'compliance committee'. 'Non-compliance is *the* major problem in therapeutics' . . .

At last the profession is getting off its high horse (easier now since the pedestal on which it stands is lower than before). Instead of 'compliance', the word 'concordance' is now coming into vogue. 'The intention is to assist the patient to make as informed a choice as possible about the diagnosis and treatment, about benefit and risk and to take full part in a therapeutic alliance. *Although reciprocal, this is an alliance in which the most important determinations are agreed to be those that are made by the patient.*' [57]

Tell Your Doctor What You Think!

People don't seem to like taking drugs at all. But if your doctor does not suggest an alternative then you need to speak up. In Newcastle upon Tyne, doctors gave standard 'quality of life' questionnaires to 75 patients who were receiving treatment for hypertension, to assess how they were feeling. They also asked the patients' doctors to assess how they felt the patients were getting along.

This would have been an interesting study in itself, but in a stroke of brilliance, they also asked the patients' *relatives* to fill out a questionnaire, to find out how *they* thought the patient was coming along.

The doctors thought the patients were doing just famously. They registered 100 percent improvement. After all, the blood pressure was adequately controlled, there was no deterioration to be found clinically and the patients did not complain about any problems. The patients on the other hand did not quite share the doctors' rosy outlook. Only 48 percent of them felt improved and 8 percent felt worse!

The relatives panned the treatment! They rated 25 percent to have suffered mild adverse changes, 45 percent to have had moderate adverse changes and 30 percent to have had severe impairment after receiving antihypertensive treatment. They reported deterioration in memory, increased worry, irritability, lower mood, loss of interest and initiative, lowered energy, less activity and hypochondria![58]

What is going on here? Doctors feel patients will not be satisfied unless they leave the consultation with a diagnosis and a prescription for a 'product' that will help them. They feel pressure from their peers to prescribe. They hear nothing back from the patient so assume everything is OK. Patients feel they should not question the authority of the doctor. Having committed themselves to a lifetime of pill popping, they put a brave face on it. The *folie à trois* begins. Doctor and patient circle each other in the *danse macabre*, urged on gleefully by the pharmaceutical rep. Only the small voice of the relatives is heard as they watch the steps, aghast.

You, the patient, are the central figure in this grotesque caper. If you don't like therapy that is potentially dangerous, costly and overpromoted, then you can break the circle, step out of the dance and be free of it. You have the right to determine your own destiny in health care. I think you will find that your doctor is likely to be in favour of this, once you have made your wishes clear. Believe it or not, many doctors, in their heart of hearts, feel uneasy about drugs. Many would prefer not to be participants in the dance themselves, but justify drugs as a 'necessary evil', because they see no viable alternative.

How necessary is this evil, really? Remember, there are many ways to bring blood pressure down. Jim is a 42-year-old rather overweight search-and-rescue officer whose blood pressure was poorly controlled even on maximal doses of ACE inhibitor. Jim's father died at the age of 62 of a heart attack and his eldest brother had a triple-bypass operation when he was in his fifties, so when Jim's blood pressure reached 160/106 I felt obliged to add a diuretic to his ACE inhibitor. However, I also strongly advised Jim to lose weight and get a more regular dose of exercise each day. After a few weeks, Jim stopped taking his diuretic as he disliked feeling dizzy every time he stood up. So my drug therapy turned out to be not such a good idea. On the other hand, by exercising regularly and cutting down on fatty foods Jim's weight has fallen from 117 to 107 kg over a three-month period. He feels very much better, and his blood pressure is now 140/90, a much more comfortable level for both Jim and his doctor.

> . . . if the initiative comes from you, if you can bring your blood pressure down by natural means, your doctor will love you for it.

The general consensus among leading doctors now is that non-pharmacological methods are the best first-line treatment in the management of mildly elevated blood pressure. This does not mean that all doctors in the field do a very good job of promoting these measures. Often they feel inadequately trained to suggest or supervise alternatives and in the end, sadly, it is much easier to reach for the prescription pad. Nevertheless, if the initiative comes from you, if you can bring your blood pressure down by natural means, your doctor will love you for it.

There is also a strong and growing feeling in medical circles that in the case of hypertension, drugs need not be taken life-long. Non-drug methods can be tried at any time, and tapering of drug therapy is not inappropriate if undertaken with the assistance of a physician. This is called 'step-down' therapy. The idea is to 'back titrate' the drugs so that the lowest possible dose that produces the desired lowering of blood pressure can be found. That way, the harmful effects of the drug

> If you have high blood
> pressure and you do not plan
> to bring your blood pressure
> down using other means . . .
> then you should go on taking
> the drugs. However, you
> should know about their
> disadvantages.

can be minimised. One study showed that after 'step-down' therapy, 26 percent of side-effects were significantly decreased and 56 percent were completely absent.[59]

Sometimes antihypertensive drugs are necessary. Undoubtedly they have saved lives, especially in severe or malignant hypertension. If I had severely high blood pressure I would take drugs until I could get it down by other means. If you have high blood pressure and you do not plan to bring your blood pressure down using other means (or if you have been unsuccessful in doing so) then you should go on taking the drugs.

However, you should know about their disadvantages. As you might not have found out about them anywhere else, I have devoted this chapter to making it clear that if there is any possible alternative, then it is worth pursuing. In the next section we plan our escape from the medical battle-zone.

SEVEN

The Great Escape from Drugs

In New Zealand we cannot afford the $100m we are already spending on antihypertensive medication and the situation must be the same in most countries. Clearly a new approach is necessary. The situation is serious and the urgency of finding a solution to what I have called the epidemiologist's dilemma is well understood within the medical profession.

Drug therapy is so central to the practice of medicine, so vigorously promoted as the 'only way', that one might assume that its widespread acceptance is the result of consensus reached by objective, free-thinking scientific minds, perhaps working in independent universities, and always with the health of the patient held uppermost. In fact, this is not the case. The discovery and development of drugs occurred, almost without exception, in the laboratories of large industrial concerns, as the eminent physician Lord Platt pointed out as long ago as 1967:

> . . . the findings are essentially the same when we look into the origins of anaesthetics, tranquillizers, vitamins, antimalarials, antihistamines, hypotensives, sex hormones and oral contraceptives. Not one originated in a department of academic medicine or therapeutics.[60]

Each one of us must decide whether we are to continue dancing to the tune called by the pharmaceutical companies and beaten out by their drummers. If I were having to take drugs I would want to escape. There are many ways to bring blood pressure down, and drugs are only one of them.

The Way Out

Among many other methods, you might bring your blood pressure down through diet, by getting more exercise, by changing your lifestyle or your job, by cutting down on salt, by learning how to manage stress or by taking more holidays. There are many books that will tell you this, as well as pamphlets written by government health departments and well-meaning community groups. Why am I writing one more book? This is because, in my view, all these publications suffer from one disadvantage. That disadvantage can be summed up in the old adage: 'One man's meat is another man's poison.' Most authorities give one set of advice to all comers. Unfortunately, what works for one person may not work for others—it might even be harmful. From my experience, I can think of only one intervention that I would regard as suitable for all—that is the technique of Transcendental Meditation. I say this because it operates on a universal level of consciousness that is common to all people. All others, including diet and exercise, operate in areas of physiology in which we differ from one another and thus need a more individualised approach. I will describe how this can be done in the pages that follow.

If I were a public health planner, facing the epidemiologist's dilemma, then, from an overall perspective I would be considering at least three ways we can extricate ourselves. The first is a way to make the mass, population-based approach really work. The aim is to lower the average levels of blood pressure by treating all hypertensives *en masse*. The answer here is to find a method that, unlike drug therapy, has no side-effects. Preferably it should have *side-benefits*. It should also be at least as effective as drugs. Then it could be recommended to anyone without fear of causing harm. Ideally, the full list of criteria would be: globally effective (meaning effective not only in bringing blood pressure down, but in improving the subjects' overall health), cost-effective, safe and available. As mentioned above, the most effective way I have found that meets these criteria is Transcendental Meditation.

The second approach is the individualised approach. Instead of giving everyone the same blanket dietary instruction, for example 'eat less salt' (which may or may not be good for an individual), we could learn to treat each person with exactly the lifestyle and dietary advice that that person needs. Of course, we would need to know a lot more about people to do this. We will look at this approach in detail in Chapter Twelve.

And the third approach? Instead of trying to treat everyone, go and find the people who are to have strokes or heart attacks and treat them only. Treat them with drugs if necessary, or better still with less damaging lifestyle interventions. The medical profession is moving in this direction, to some degree at least, by identifying 'at risk' groups. As the editor of the *British Medical Journal* said recently: '. . . with the wisdom of hindsight much of our response [to the problem of heart disease] looks unintelligent: treating people, regardless of their . . . risk, when they cross a particular magic line of blood pressure or lipid concentration.'[61] However, as well as understanding how people behave as groups and sub-groups it would be even more helpful to know about what makes *each person special*, for then we could pinpoint the individuals who are going to have a stroke or heart attack. Furthermore, we could then uniquely tailor our diet and life-style advice to him or her alone. This would require a much more sophisticated method of early diagnosis than we have at present and we will investigate this idea also in Chapter Twelve.

PART THREE

Perfect Blood Pressure, Perfect Health

EIGHT

The Quest for Wholeness

As far as Cresswell Jones is concerned he has stopped worrying because his pills have started working and his blood pressure is now back to normal levels! True, the first lot were ineffective and made him feel very tired, but Dr Feldstein prescribed another sort. It works! No side-effects! He feels fine! He's getting on top of this blood pressure thing, and that night while preparing for bed, he says so to his wife, Ellen, who at that moment is sitting up in bed, hair curlers in place, absorbed in a gardening magazine. 'I think I am getting the better of this hypertension,' he says. 'I've got perfect blood pressure!' She looks up momentarily. 'That's good, I suppose. But what does perfect mean? Does that mean you're perfectly well?'

'What does perfect mean, Ellen? What a question! It means ... well it means that I don't have high blood pressure any more. So I'm OK!' 'You had high blood pressure,' responds Ellen. 'That means there must have been something wrong with you somewhere. How do you know those little pink tablets are making it any better? Maybe they're just masking the problem. If you ask me, I think those tablets are making you tired!' 'B-but, hang on Ellen, the doctor said I might have a cardiovascular accident. That's a stroke. You don't want me to have a stroke do you? And strokes can be caused by blood pressure. So I've got to take these pills. It's probably a bit like wearing seat-belts. You

might never have a road accident. But it's just as well to be prepared.'

That's the worst of Ellen, he thinks to himself. She knows nothing about technical things, but always seems to hit the spot when she questions you about them. Cresswell decides not to pursue the matter. Ellen has in any case returned to her magazine. He feels all at sea again. When you think about it, seat-belts don't harm you. There's no risk in popping them on. They don't give you crook kidneys, or mess up your blood cells or make you feel light-headed. Not like pills. Why risk damaging yourself for something that probably isn't going to happen? He feels the old anxiety creeping back. His wife emerges from her article (on French tarragon), gives him a steady look and says: 'Cresswell, I don't want you to have a stroke. But something doesn't feel right to me. Those pills might be bringing your blood pressure down, but how do you know they are really curing you? You might end up having a stroke anyway, if the problem is still there. Honestly, Cresswell, I think you're looking more stressed and worried than before you ever saw that doctor.'

When he gets to work next day, Cresswell puts aside the absorbing end-of-year accounts for Springer, Fawcett, Parsonage and Hodge Ltd, clears his desk and takes a long hard look at himself. He's not really feeling all that well. The jogging seems to take it out of him somehow. Things have not improved in the household since the onset of winter. The caravan leaked and was cold and he has had to give up his home office to provide his daughter with a bedroom. The llama has some kind of foot infection. Ellen is not herself either. She looks pale and strained. F. F. F. & Q. has been busy and he is working 60-hour weeks. His mind is always full of thoughts, yet he has trouble concentrating. He has started smoking again. He finds himself thinking about tomorrow instead of thinking about today. At the end of the day he feels exhausted, yet he does not seem to have achieved very much. He wonders whether he is suffering from stress. Ellen has noticed too and feels concerned.

You may have normal blood pressure but is it perfect? It is easy to imagine, once a pill is 'working', that the job is done. Yet, while Cresswell's blood pressure is 'controlled', he is not feeling well. Part of him has been cured, but most of him has not. He senses that he is not fully healthy. Since Dr Feldstein had told him his blood pressure is

now 'normal' (he meant 'usual'),
Cresswell assumed that it was normal in
the sense of ideal. A little learning is a
dangerous thing, and Cresswell Jones has
become a victim of fragmented knowledge. Ellen has put her finger on a

> Perfect blood pressure is the kind you have when you are completely healthy.

fundamental problem. We might bring the pressure down, but if this
simply masks an underlying problem, then the dangers we were trying
to avoid—heart attacks and strokes—might occur anyway. The fact is
that many hundreds of thousands of people have died from heart
attacks and strokes with blood pressure that was completely 'normal'.

In reality, medicine has failed Cresswell. In moving to correct that
small wedge of him that is represented by his blood pressure, medicine
has failed to take into account the well-being of Cresswell as a whole.
Drug therapy, while it may bring blood pressure down, does not get
to the root of the problem; it does not address the total Cresswell.

Earlier we implied that we were not satisfied with blood pressure
that was just 'normal'. We are seeking blood pressure that is the 'best',
hence the name of the book. Perfect blood pressure is the kind you
you have when you are completely healthy.

Clearly there are many factors that contribute to a heart attack or a
stroke besides high blood pressure. We have seen that medicine has
identified a few of them, high blood cholesterol, smoking and diabetes
for example, but at best these risk factors predict who is to have a
medical disaster in only about 50 percent of cases. In the other 50
percent we get it wrong. We do not have the complete picture, some
vital pieces of the jigsaw puzzle are not in their places. We could move
the pieces around trying one after another to see which fits where.
This is the line medicine is pursuing. We could, however, take a
different tack altogether, and this is the approach I wish to explore in
the remainder of this book.

The approach I suggest could be compared with finding the box
that the jigsaw puzzle came in and getting an idea of what fits where
by looking at the picture on the front. The picture gives us an overview,
a view of the jigsaw puzzle 'as a whole'. Our problem is that we have
not addressed Cresswell as a whole, we have only addressed parts of

him. Is there some way we could get the 'big picture', *perhaps even without having to attend to all the component Cresswell parts*? We want to help Cresswell as a whole. Is this possible? Is it possible to know about wholeness, study it, even enhance wholeness?

The idea of wholeness in relation to medicine is not new. The word health means wholeness. It is derived from the Greek word, *holos*. Holos is also the root for our words hale and holy. A World Health Organization definition, originally proposed in 1946, states that health is 'a state of complete physical, mental and social well-being, and not merely the absence of disease'. The idea behind such a spiritually uplifting definition has never disappeared entirely from the profession.

The study of wholeness is now one of the most exciting fields at the cutting edge of medicine, although we should not be surprised that such a global endeavour has involved many other fields as well.

In the next few pages, let's take a brief tour of what could be called 'global theories', theories of wholeness.

One of the first to appear in recent times is known as 'general systems theory' with which the scholar Ludwig von Bertalanffy is generally associated. Bertalanffy states:

> The only goal of science appeared to be analytical, i.e., the splitting up of reality into ever smaller units and the isolation of individual causal trains. Thus, physical reality was split up ... one sort of bacterium produces this or that disease, mental elements are lined up, like the beads in a string of pearls ...[62]

Von Bertalanffy became puzzled that this sort of approach 'appeared to neglect or deny just what is essential in the phenomenon of life'. To understand life one had to understand not just the parts of an organism, but how those parts come together to form a living whole. His general systems theory, designed to explain how things interact with each other 'as a whole', had an immense impact. In the mechanistic 1950s it filled a void in the minds of many, penetrating popular thinking and the jargon of the marketplace. Suddenly 'systems' became a catchword. Even today, no self-respecting business can be without its 'systems analyst' or 'systems engineer' and including 'systems' in the name of your firm ('Software Systems', 'Electrical Systems', 'Plumbing Systems') seems to suggest expertise.

In the field known as cybernetics, the principle of feedback, by which a mechanical system can regulate itself, was proving fruitful to understand how things act 'as a whole'. It explained the ways in which a living system maintains the constancy of its internal environment (the *milieu intérieur* of Claude Bernard). In much the same way as the thermometer in a hot water cylinder feeds information back to a controller controlling the input of heat to the cylinder, thus keeping the water at an even temperature, the body came to be understood to keep such vital factors as temperature, blood glucose and blood pressure even by similar means. On the other hand, positive or explosive feedback could be seen to explain certain situations in which the body goes awry, malignant hypertension being an example, in which increasing blood pressure seems to further drive the blood pressure up, instead of down. It is the information that is vital. We now talk about the 'information age', indicating how completely this line of thought is recognised in popular parlance.

Others took up the quest for wholeness. The physicist David Bohm published an important book called *Wholeness and the Implicate Order*,[33] in which he explored the idea of a hidden order 'behind the scenes', a field of wholeness underlying the gross phenomena of life. The Nobel Laureate chemist Ilya Prigogene brilliantly formulated his ideas on the 'non-linear dynamics' of living systems in which he moved to explain the multiple interacting forces that act as a whole to create a living system. Two disciplines that emerged independently are, in fact, closely related. These are nonlinear dynamics and chaos theory.

Non-linear Dynamics and Chaos Theory

Non-linear dynamics is a fascinating, mushrooming science which encompasses many fields from medicine to economics to sociology. Among the many insights it yields is that the chemistry of the human body, as in all living systems, is constantly changing and in many respects is seemingly chaotic. Yet within that chaos is an underlying order that echoes the 'implicate order' of David Bohm. Your blood sugar is not kept at a constant level, it fluctuates within certain limits in a puzzlingly random manner. Your heart beat may seem steady, but it also fluctuates 'randomly'. Your blood pressure is no exception. It rises and falls literally with every heart beat. The constancy of Claude Bernard's *milieu intérieur* is, on closer inspection, not so constant after all.

Paradoxically, within this seeming haphazardness is the very essence of health. In fact it is now generally accepted by 'chaologists' that a too constant *milieu intérieur* is downright dangerous. If your heart beat becomes too regular *then you are actually on the path to a heart attack*. Within the random fluctuations of chaos there is a hidden order. Lose those fluctuations and you lose your health. Health is not a rigid state. The state of wholeness includes flux, movement and change. Though this change is seemingly random, a hidden, higher level of orderliness governs it.

Thus change becomes a prerequisite for stability. But this is not the stability of fixedness, it is not the stability of a rock. To be truly stable allows for adaptability, flexibility and growth. A spinning top can only stay upright by virtue of its movement. If it did not spin it would fall over immediately and reach a state of equilibrium on its side, dead. It needs to spin to maintain itself in the upright position. Yet while it is spinning, try to push it off balance. Your move will be instantly resisted and the top will assume its upright position once again.

Our physiology, like the top, from a chemical point of view is in an unstable state. Just like the top, we need change to stay stable. Change, progress, flexibility keep us alive. If we become inflexible, unable to flow with the changing universe, then, like the top, we fall over on our sides. The more we can be like the top and flexibly resist the changes in our environment, the more we are truly healthy. In other words if we get a shove from the environment (called in chaos theory, a perturbation), whether it be a nasty fall or a flu virus, the more flexible we are then the more healthy we are, and the more we can come up smiling, like the top.

We are learning from the science of non-linear dynamics and its partner chaos theory, that the seemingly random changes that occur in the body are part of a 'higher-level' orderliness that allows us to stay 'light on our feet'. We can thus keep our physiological equanimity in the face of a changing environment that threatens to throw us out of kilter. The more we can keep in touch with the 'higher-level' orderliness, the more healthy we can be.

If flexibility is a prerequisite for health, how much should we be trying to 'fix' our blood pressure at a certain steady level? Doctors often talk about their patients' blood pressure being 'well controlled'. Is this necessarily a good thing? Can we overdo it? Could it be that nature has a design in the fluctuations of our blood pressure that is not immediately apparent? Perhaps we need to be co-operating with, rather than controlling nature. Perhaps we need to find ways to get in touch with nature in its wholeness to access those higher levels of orderliness. Could it be that 'control of nature' is 'a phrase conceived in arrogance, born of the Neanderthal age of biology and philosophy', as Rachel Carson put it.

The degree to which the body is integrated, whole, staying 'light on its feet', changing, yet constant overall, can now be measured mathematically. It is usually referred to as the degree of 'chaos' within a system. This system might include the heart rate, or blood pressure or blood glucose levels or any seemingly random physiological measurements. The word 'chaos' is a little unfortunate, since, as we have seen, apparent 'chaos' is a symptom of higher-level orderliness. Wholeness would be, I think, a better word. However, 'chaos' has stuck in the scientific community and is unlikely to be easily abandoned. Chaos theory has found its way deeply into our culture and is found in an extraordinarily wide diversity of fields. It has been used to decrease the noise in a telephone line, explain traffic flow in a city, predict changes in the stock-market and test the looseness of a patient's prosthetic hip, as well as predict who is likely to have a heart attack.

At the cutting edge of Western thought, this theory is all about wholeness. It tells us that each aspect of the human body relates to the whole of the body and indeed the whole of the universe. A 'chaotic' system is one in which, although the parts appear to move in a random way, they are actually dancing to a grandly choreographed score.

When 'chaos' is lost, then the parts lose their connection with the whole. The actions of a single regiment in an army could seem chaotic to an onlooker if the grand intentions of their general were unknown. If the regiment were to lose communication with the general and start to make its own decisions, while it may look to be behaving in a more orderly fashion, it would, like a bee without its queen, simply be acting robotically, having lost its overall purpose. Loss of 'chaotic properties' (increasingly autonomous 'robotic' behaviour of a part) has been discovered in many disease states including cancer,[63] diabetes[64] and brain function disorder.[65]

Where flexibility, chaos, wholeness and integration do not exist, disease occurs. Atherosclerosis, the disease of arteries behind both heart attacks and strokes, does not occur uniformly along the artery. It tends to build up at very specific points, such as where an artery divides or bifurcates. One very interesting line of research now suggests that this may be because blood slows down or 'pools' in these areas. In these areas there is a lack of change. The pumping effect of the pulse does not reach them and the usual movement of the artery wall in and out (shear stress) with each beat of the heart does not occur.[66] With lack of movement comes disease. (This is particularly arresting since whether the blood pools in this way or not probably depends, among other things, on the wave-form of the pulse and how it interacts with the reflected waves coming back off the arterial walls. The character of the pulse is something that has interested doctors for centuries, and, as we shall see, is of primary consideration in Maharishi's Vedic Approach to Health.)

In the cardiac arena, a loss of chaotic property, a loss of connection with the whole, can be seen in the heart rate of people in heart failure[67] and obese subjects.[68] It seems that these people are beginning to lose touch with the 'higher-level ordering properties' that keep them in kilter with the totality of their physiology. Their bodies are starting to function like an automaton, without reference to 'head office'. When any system ceases to function as a whole, whether it be a family, a business, or an army, then difficulties are likely to occur. Of course the most obvious example of autonomous behaviour in which parts of the body cease to take instructions from the whole is in the cancer cell.

Non-linear dynamics and chaos theory enable us to apprehend mathematically the behaviour of a system as a whole *without necessarily knowing about all the parts*. It is clear why this type of thinking has attracted such energy and interest among research scientists. It is near to impossible to understand each of the trillions of chemical reactions that occur in the human physiology, so a method to understand how it works 'as a whole', without having to know all about each chemical reaction, has enormous potential.

We have been able to identify a few predictive factors for heart disease—hypertension, smoking, high cholesterol and so forth—but we know there are many that we are unaware of yet. Indeed we suspect that some are so subtle we may never be able to know them. Maybe by thinking less of the parts and learning to understand how the whole behaves, we can get round this problem. Already non-linear dynamics is being used to predict whether patients who have had heart attacks will go on to have a cardiac arrhythmia, just by studying their heart rate. No other variables are used in this prediction, just the changes in the rate at which the heart beats. From the degree of 'chaotic behaviour' (or lack of it in this case) a prediction can be made about the functioning of the whole system.[69]

Can non-linear dynamics be applied in hypertension? A loss of heart rate variability (loss of randomness, loss of 'chaos') has been noted in essential hypertension by a group of Japanese researchers.[70] It seems very likely that high blood pressure, blood pressure that is not fluctuating downwards as often as it should, indeed represents a loss of higher-level orderliness within the cardiovascular system. A loss of higher-level orderliness is just another way of saying loss of wholeness, loss of connection with the whole.

The idea that fragmentation from the whole is the root of disease can be traced to antiquity. In Maharishi's Vedic Approach to Health it is given a name. It is called *pragya aparadh*, and we will return to it in detail in a later chapter.

We began this chapter by recognising that in treating Cresswell Jones' blood pressure alone we were simply masking the problem, rather than getting to the root of it. We accepted that simply restoring the blood pressure to normal levels could leave the underlying problem unsolved, and we suspected that somehow the problem involved the whole of Cresswell. Now we find from the most advanced scientific theory that, in fact, to really get to the root of Cresswell's problem, we *must* consider Cresswell as a whole. If we could 'defragment Cresswell', recreate the connection of the parts of Cresswell to the whole of Cresswell, then perhaps Cresswell's blood pressure would correct itself, just as a soldier falls into line when he has finally received instructions from his general. Moreover, since all the other parts of the jigsaw puzzle that is Cresswell would find their proper places, Cresswell would not simply have normal blood pressure, he would have ideal blood pressure, perfect blood pressure, the sort you have when you do not have heart attacks or strokes, because you are completely healthy.

How to get in touch with the general? How to restore physiological co-ordination? Systems theory, information theory, non-linear dynamics and chaos theory are all highly exciting, rapidly progressing areas which propel us out of the reductivist rut and promise to open up much deeper understandings of how the parts of our bodies function in relation to the whole. Nevertheless, for all their power, these 'global theories' are still no more than intellectual representations of reality. Chaos theory may 'map' reality very well, but in the end it is just a map. A map is an abstraction, it can never be reality itself. A theory, such as chaos theory, can help us in our understanding, but it does not, in itself, allow us to *do* anything useful *with wholeness itself*. We might be able to predict who is going to have the arrhythmia, but stopping it from happening is another matter. Knowing *about* wholeness does not allow us to *create* wholeness, or enhance it. We must not mistake the map for the territory. The mathematics of wholeness simply describes wholeness and is probably the wrong tool to use if we want to *become* more whole. For that we will need to look more deeply.

Becoming More Whole

If, as implied by chaos theory, essential hypertension results from loss of contact with a higher degree of physiological orderliness then, if we can somehow reconnect to that level, our blood pressure should go down. Not only that, but since higher levels of orderliness imply integration and wholeness, which, in turn, imply health, we should feel better in all sorts of other ways besides.

This is a big thought. If we can do this, then we are standing modern medicine on its head. Instead of studying the parts to create a better whole, we create a better whole and the parts fall into line. It could be very much easier.

Can this be done? Yes, but it requires a different sort of knowledge from the intellectual kind that simply describes

> ... we are standing modern medicine on its head. Instead of studying the parts to create a better whole, we create a better whole and the parts fall into line.

wholeness. We have to be able to create wholeness from deep within.

Intellectual knowledge alone can be dry and detached from life. The poet Samuel Taylor Coleridge was obviously aware of this:

> I have known some men who have been rationally educated as it is styled. They were marked by a microscopic acuteness, but when they looked at great things, all became blank and they saw nothing.

There are different ways of knowing. You can know something deeply or superficially. Knowledge can be an abstract representation, a sort of caricature, or it can be a loving identification with its object, an intimacy with its most subtle detail. In the former you know with your mind and in the latter you know with your heart.

Most mainstream medical knowledge involves knowledge of abstractions. This kind of knowledge has its own value, yet if it were our only knowledge then we would be the more impoverished for that. The truth of a proposition can be accepted without making the slightest difference to how a person feels about it or how they live or act. I have met many a philosopher who with his or her 'microscopic acuteness' can argue persuasively for proposition A, then, in the next breath, and with perfect equanimity, argue equally persuasively for the opposite proposition, not-A. Many lawyers can do the same and doctors often have a reputation for being overly 'clinical'. Clearly the *import* of what they are saying has made not the slightest impression on them nor is it perceived to have any relevance to life itself.

The internationally recognised doyen of academic general practice, Dr Ian McWhinney describes three levels of knowing: the physical, the mental and the transcendental.[71]

On the physical level, knowledge is sensory. This is the level at which much of medicine operates, the level of empiricism. Of course doctors, especially general practitioners and psychiatrists, have to know about what patients are thinking and feeling. This is knowledge on the mental level. It is subjective knowledge, but important nevertheless for it puts us in touch with our patients' inner world.

> In gaining transcendental knowledge, not only does one know *about* wholeness, one learns to *be whole*.

Transcendental knowledge has been recognised by all the great religions and schools of philosophy. It is the distilled wisdom of the ages, defined by Leibnitz as the 'perennial philosophy', yet for thousands of years it has been the least understood. About this level of knowledge, McWhinney has this to say: 'Knowledge at this level cannot be expressed in words or attained by the intellect. We know a person has attained it because it transforms the whole personality.'

Transcendental knowledge is the knowledge of wholeness. In gaining transcendental knowledge, not only does one know *about* wholeness, one learns to *be whole*. As McWhinney says, this is the knowledge that transforms.

Many Western writers have reached the brink of transcendental knowledge yet, having recognised its importance, seem unsure about how to proceed in developing it. For Freud it was the 'oceanic experience', but he gives no clue as to how it could be elicited. This is because for thousands of years the knowledge of how to create transcendental knowledge has been missing from our Western culture.

Fortunately, while von Bertalanffy, Prigogene and others were carrying out their important work, a deeper yet very practical system for gaining transcendental knowledge was being revived and presented to the West. This system, called Transcendental Meditation, was being carefully prepared and unfolded by Maharishi Mahesh Yogi. I will introduce it in the next chapter.

NINE

Coming Back Home

Transcendental Knowledge—Maharishi's Vedic Approach to Health

One morning at breakfast, Cresswell, moodily munching his cornflakes, is wondering partly about how to meet an important deadline by the end of the day, and partly about how to deal with the young upstart Damien Stent who has joined the firm. He would like to give that fellow a piece of his mind! Vaguely he hears Ellen, who has been reading the paper, say: 'Cresswell, there's an article here saying that 20 minutes of Transcendental Meditation twice a day is good for your blood pressure. Maybe that's something for you.' These words at any rate impinge on Cresswell's eardrums. What penetrates to the essential Cresswell is, from an information point of view, a degraded signal: Ellen is talking. About blood pressure. No use because Ellen doesn't know about blood pressure. She's lovely, Ellen, but not technical. Meditation! What next? Mechanically, Cresswell returns to his cornflakes. 'That's interesting, dear,' he says.

The word Veda means knowledge. The Veda is a timeless knowledge, carefully preserved in India by a long, 5000-year oral tradition. In the form in which we find it, it consists of sequences of Sanskrit sounds that are meticulously memorised and recited by experts known as Vedic Pundits. Pundit families, in which these sequences are passed down from father to son, are to be found throughout India. Over the

years I have come to realise that in bringing to light the true significance of these usually unintelligible sounds, the contribution that
Maharishi Mahesh Yogi has made stands as a turning point in the
evolution of human affairs. His deep understanding of the Vedic
tradition, gained from long years of study under his own Vedic Master,
has allowed him to distill its essence, yet his orthodox Western training
and familiarity with the Western mind has allowed him to present it
in a way that is eminently practical and useful to hurried and harried
people in the West. It is now increasingly recognised that his work
places him as a foremost scientist and scholar of our time.

While the Veda has been revered in India, its interpretation has
been puzzling and difficult. Translation of the Sanskrit sounds
yields an abstruse series of words somewhat resembling poetry.
According to Maharishi, the translations are of lesser importance.
What is important is the actual sound of the words themselves. Rather
as the sounds of a computer sending data through its modem have
significance to another computer, the Vedic sounds are of the utmost
significance when interpreted correctly. According to Maharishi they
describe, or rather are, the fundamental patterns that form our
universe. Maharishi describes the Veda as the 'blueprint of creation', a
kind of users' manual for the universe. According to the Vedic
tradition, the Veda contains in seed form all the impulses of natural
law that give rise to what we perceive around us. At the core of the
Veda and at the heart of the universe stands transcendental knowledge,
the knowledge of wholeness.

In this short account it is not possible to convey the full significance
of Maharishi's insight or the scope of its application. Maharishi
himself has written extensively on the application of the Veda in key
areas of society,[72, 73] and others have written valuable commentaries.[74]
It will be enough to know that Maharishi has distilled from the Veda a
powerful technique which allows us to experience wholeness directly.
This is the technique of Transcendental Meditation. Transcendental
Meditation is an eminently practical way for anybody to enjoy the fruit
of Vedic knowledge without necessarily having to study its myriad
aspects. In spite of the abstractions we have been considering, the
actual technique turns out to be very simple, so simple that it can be

learned by almost anyone, regardless of age, educational background, beliefs or abilities. It requires no previous experience nor does it require any prior interest in meditation or Vedic knowledge. Hence Transcendental Meditation is enjoyed by literally millions of people, worldwide.

These people have learned Transcendental Meditation for a wide variety of reasons. They may have learned it to help them relax, to find inner peace and happiness, to enjoy greater energy and stamina, to perform better at their work or in their sport, to improve their health, to enjoy more rewarding social relationships or to build confidence and self-esteem.

> . . . the actual technique turns out to be very simple, so simple that it can be learned by almost anyone, regardless of age, educational background or abilities.

The purpose of this book is to help bring our blood pressure down to safe levels. I am emphasising Transcendental Meditation in this regard because, of all the non-pharmacological interventions that I have studied, Transcendental Meditation is in my opinion the most universally useful and effective. Transcendental Meditation has been shown in randomised trials to bring high blood pressure down as effectively as drugs. Indeed, it does a great deal more than that. Because it is creating wholeness within the individual, it creates health on a broad front. Often people will learn this technique solely for the purpose of bringing their blood pressure down. This is a perfectly valid reason. They are then surprised and delighted to find it brings them many other useful benefits as well. Rather than having side-effects as drugs do, it has side-benefits. Margot provides an example of this from my case notes.

Margot is a 56-year-old retired caregiver originally from the North of England who was referred to my practice by her own GP. She had recently been through some distressing family upheavals associated with their emigration to New Zealand. When she presented to my clinic she suffered from headaches, incessant worried thoughts and insomnia. She had had a tendency to backache since attempting to lift a patient twenty years earlier, and her blood pressure was remaining obstinately in the mildly elevated range in spite of taking a maximal dose of an antihypertensive drug. Two weeks before her instruction in Transcendental Meditation her blood pressure was 150/96, and five readings taken in the four previous months had been in the range 142–170/88–100.

'I wish I had found out about this a long time ago!'

We are all different and we all react to the new experience of transcending thought differently. Margot's initial reaction was to notice what I call the 'holiday reaction', the sudden tiredness that comes to busy people sometimes when they finally stop. I encouraged her to get as much extra rest as possible. Her body was gratefully taking the rest it had been denied for months—probably years. Within a few days her energy returned to well above its previous levels. 'I am amazed at how much more I am doing,' she said. 'I'm not putting things off, I'm doing them then and there!' Margot also noticed she was finding it easier to get out of bed. 'No more thinking "I'll just have a few more minutes!"' Her sleep improved. 'Before I had the odd night sleeping well, now not sleeping well is the exception.' Whereas a trip to the shopping mall had been enough to precipitate her back pain, this was no longer occurring. With the help of some self-massage known in Maharishi's Vedic Approach to Health as *abhyanga*, her headaches were improving. Her blood pressure one week after learning Transcendental Meditation was 146/82, after two weeks, 138/78 and after three weeks 140/75. In discussion with her doctor I first halved, then withdrew her dose of medication altogether. Her blood pressure, when she was last seen, was 138/84. Margot's comment: 'I wish I had found out about this a long time ago!'

In the next few pages I will try to give you an insight into how the technique works. When you try the technique yourself, you will find that it is very easy. This is because it will seem very natural to you. It is easier in the end to simply taste a strawberry than describe the taste to someone else!

How many thoughts do you have each day? Lots? One psychologist is said to have estimated that we have 60,000 thoughts per day! (He also said that 90 percent are the same ones we had yesterday!) Nevertheless thoughts are indispensable to life. You could not be reading this book without a succession of thoughts, nor could you have decided to get up this morning, get dressed and start your day.

Many people find their thoughts so dominant that they seem to be no longer masters of them. Rather, their thoughts have mastered them. Thoughts seem to have assumed their own direction, their own lives and have, as it were, 'minds of their own'. A noisy contingent of determined thoughts seems to parade along the main thoroughfare of the mind, persistent enough during the day, but becoming downright unruly when their 'owner' tries to get to sleep! Most people will recognise the experience in which one intends to think about a task at hand and one's thoughts, taking a puckish life of their own, concern themselves with entirely unrelated subjects. We would like to study a text, or attend to a lecture, and we go 'off the air', thinking perhaps about our holiday. Like Cresswell when being addressed by his wife, we might miss something important. The more we try to discipline the mind, the more we try to bring these unruly thoughts into line, the more, like mischievous children, they skip away to their own devices.

Thoughts are a part of us, yet these particular parts are not responding properly to the whole. We have lost mastery over our thoughts; the part has gained the kind of autonomy that should properly be allowed only to the whole. Once again we come across the problem of fragmentation. What we experience in the wayward nature of our day-to-day thoughts looks uncannily similar to the unhealthy loss of higher-level orderliness we identified in twentieth-century theories of chaos. We could call this 'inappropriate autonomy', the part getting 'too big for its boots' and assuming a status it does not deserve. This is a loss of wholeness. We lose our own integrity to the caprices of those parts of us we call our thoughts. If we wish to recreate wholeness, it should be no surprise that the technique to do that involves somehow getting behind our thoughts to restore our own autonomy. As mentioned earlier, in Maharishi's Vedic Approach to Health the inappropriate autonomy that our thoughts assume for themselves is given a name. It is called pragya aparadh. So it is pragya aparadh that we must somehow overcome.

Pragya Aparadh

Pragya aparadh literally means 'mistake of the intellect'. The function of the intellect, according to Maharishi, is to discriminate. Accordingly, the intellect is like a knife that divides and fragments. Knives are very useful things. So is the intellect, provided we remember that it is only a tool. We make categories for ease of communication and as a kind of shorthand. But we must remember that we do this as a convenience only, and that our 'view' of the world is, in the final analysis, arbitrary. If we ascribe the furniture of our shorthand world a reality that is independent of the total world, then we are making a mistake. Thoughts are vital, yet they can ensnare us into pragya aparadh. We are apt to forget that everything is connected. Things are fluid. Everything merges into everything else; the boundaries are only as sharp as we have chosen to make them.

Pragya aparadh is more than just an intellectual error, the kind of confusion that philosophers delight in confronting their opponents with. This is no superficial mistake on the level of intellectual debate, it is a fundamental error of perception that affects us deeply in all aspects of our lives. So deeply does it affect us that pragya aparadh is seen by Vedic Science to be the root cause of all illness and suffering. It is at this subtle level of mental functioning that the conditions for disease are set.

This is precisely the same concept we encountered in chaos theory. The universe is fluid, whole and interconnected. When parts such as the heart, or a group of cells, or our thoughts cease to operate in connection with the whole then the stage for ill-health is set.

How can we overcome pragya aparadh? To do this, we need to withdraw from the compelling influence of the boundaries, the categories of thought that we have created. So entrenched are we in these categories that it can seem quite difficult to detach from them. I am referring here to our everyday thoughts. For most of us, the intellect is busy, busy, constantly on the go, in a way that for many is almost out of control.

Concentration and Contemplation Are Not the Way to Go

We need a way that we can somehow 'step back' from our thoughts and overcome their dominance. We need to be able to become the masters of our thoughts. Since the intellect got us into this problem, could the intellect get us out? Many people have tried to use their intellectual powers to somehow 'think themselves out of their thoughts'. You may have tried yourself. Have you ever tried to make your mind go blank? Was it easy? Or perhaps you have tried keeping the mind steady, always on a particular thought, or on a candle flame. Did you not find it hard? The problem is that as soon as you have the thought 'I must keep a blank mind', you have a thought! Concentrating on a blank mind is rather like trying to pull yourself up by your bootstraps. Such a mental impossibility we can call a concentration technique. In practice, concentration exercises lead to frustration and feelings of inadequacy among those who try them. This is unfortunate, because according to Maharishi, concentration techniques are a misinterpretation of what the word 'meditation' really means. Only slightly less unrewarding are techniques in which people are advised to still the mind by thinking a 'good' thought, such as 'peace', or they might try to think of beautiful scenery or a happy experience they have had. The trouble with this approach is that once again you are left with thoughts, this time about peace, scenery or your happy experience. Maharishi again differentiates these 'contemplation' techniques from correct meditation.

These two methods of attempting to free ourselves from the binding influence of thoughts, concentration and contemplation, are what occur to most people when they think of meditation. Concentration and contemplation seem to be logical and obvious approaches. The intellect thinks they should work. But when you try them, they turn out to be frustrating and unrewarding. In practice, they simply do not work.

Unfortunately, since most people associate either concentration or contemplation with meditation, meditation has become thought of as something rather impractical, a nice idea perhaps, but since it is not very effective, of no real value in the world.

Both concentration and contemplation are completely and utterly different from Transcendental Meditation. These methods have been corruptions in our understanding of meditation. In fact, the ability to transcend thought is a simple, natural process that is inherent in all of us.

Psychologists tell us that we use only a very small proportion of our full mental potential, perhaps five or ten percent. Certainly we could be using a great deal more. The reason we are using such a miserable portion of the mind is precisely because for most of us, the mind is chronically overactive.

Maharishi often compares the mind to a body of water, such as a lake (see Figure 2). A lake has an active level at the top, but it also has a quiet, silent depth. In the same way, the mind has an active surface level, but hidden within each one of us is a quiet silent area. If we could experience this, then we would be experiencing our most simple, least complicated, state of awareness. This state of awareness is called pure consciousness. It is also just you. It is you in your simplest, least complicated, most integrated, most 'whole' state. Since it is just you, it is also referred to as the Self.

Coming Back Home

Transcendental Meditation allows us to dive into the 'lake of the mind' and reach this quiet, silent area at its depth. Although we are aware of thousands of thoughts each day, on the turbulent level of life, what we are generally not aware of is that each of these thoughts started out as a tiny bubble at the bottom of the pond. We do not become conscious of them until they reach the top. This suggests a way to reach pure · consciousness, if we know how to go about it. It is possible, in a natural way, for the mind to experience finer and finer levels of thought (smaller and smaller bubbles in the analogy), until the finest level of thought is transcended and the mind is just left with itself, at the source of thought, in the state of pure awareness. This process is called transcending, and hence Maharishi's name for the technique that brings it about, Transcendental Meditation.

Having around 60,000 thoughts per day is exhausting. The mind feels trapped in the boundaries of thoughts and tires of the incessant activity. As it approaches the state of pure consciousness, the mind is progressively freed from these boundaries. Experience of thought becomes more abstract and unbounded until finally it is completely

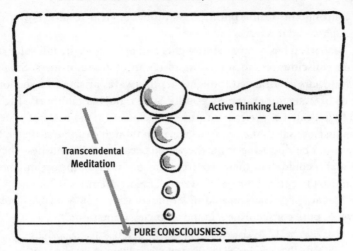

Figure 2: Energy and Happiness

The mind can be compared to a body of water such as a lake. It has an active level at the top, yet it also has a silent depth below. This most settled state of mind is called pure consciousness. We are all aware of thoughts at the active, more turbulent level. We are less aware that each thought is like a tiny bubble that starts out small and gets bigger as it comes up. By progressively refining thought (transcending) we can access an unlimited field of energy and happiness at the source of thought, pure consciousness. This is the technique of Transcendental Meditation.

unbounded. In this state the mind is deeply rested and, as a result, emerges from meditation replenished and refreshed. A settled 'feet on the ground' experience that accompanies this is a natural result of the mind becoming more integrated within itself. It has been described by many as a feeling of 'coming back home'.

Powerful Thoughts

Not only does the mind achieve deep rest during meditation; in the experience of transcendental consciousness a great deal of untangling and reintegration is going on. In the state of wholeness or pure consciousness, all the turbulent excitement of the thinking process settles down. Thoughts that emerge after this experience are thoughts that are strong and germane. They are the thoughts we want to have, not the unruly ones that seemed, willy-nilly, to pop up before. They are thoughts that will create the world we want to see. Because they are strong and to the point, these thoughts yield results. Powerful thoughts lead to success in life.

Maharishi has compared thoughts that arise from the full value of pure consciousness to waves on an ocean of consciousness. Small, choppy, unco-ordinated thoughts are like waves arising in a shallow body of water, for example a puddle. Such thoughts cannot rise high. If, by repeated experience of pure consciousness, the body of water can increase say to the size of a lake, then thoughts can be stronger. If we could be operating from the whole ocean of consciousness then thoughts could draw their base from the total body of the ocean. They could act like tidal waves and sweep all before them.

Maharishi gives us an inkling of the power that is available at the level of pure consciousness in the following quotation:

> Consciousness in the individual is that area where the totality of life is located. The body, the mind and all the different subtler values of the mind that are called intellect, ego, and so on—they are all contained in the structure of consciousness, the Self.
>
> If we know how to operate on that subtle level of consciousness, then we know how to administer the activity of all creation. The field of matter and thought can be handled precisely and just as we wish from that level of subtle awareness which we call simplest state of awareness. Because we now have the knowledge of the simplest form of awareness and the dynamics of how it can function from within its own value, we have been able to open up a field of all possibilities to human life. The human mind in the settled state is a field of all possibilities.[73]

The experience of pure consciousness is not just an idea, not just another thought among the day's 60,000. It is not even a nice mood or emotion. Pure consciousness is a deep experience of one's inner being, the ground state of the mind. The mind is experiencing, not a thought, not a mood, nor any other 'thing'. The mind has taken a 180 degree turn and is now experiencing *itself*, its own unbounded nature. Pure consciousness is not intellectual knowledge. It is not knowledge that can be 'compartmentalised'. It is not the knowledge that can be examined during the philosopher's working hours and forgotten about during the weekend. This is knowledge that endures. As Dr McWhinney said, transcendental knowledge is knowledge that transforms.

As might be expected from a technique specifically designed to create wholeness, studies have shown benefits from practising Transcendental Meditation in an extremely broad range of areas, including not only mental well-being, but physical health as well. The first scientist to study the physiological effects of practising Transcendental Meditation was Robert Keith Wallace. Keith Wallace took as his PhD thesis the physiology of the 'fourth state of consciousness', pure consciousness (the other three being waking, dreaming and sleeping). In his book, Wallace describes presenting his PhD to a group of senior research scientists and medical doctors in the late 1960s, a considerable act of bravery in a medical arena that at that time seemed an impregnable fortress of extreme materialism.

> I wanted this audience to understand that this was a turning point in the history of mankind. Two divergent streams of knowledge were converging. On the one hand, through the objective approach of modern science we were delving into the deepest layers of life and matter . . . In physics we were on the verge of arriving at a single unified theory of matter and energy—Einstein's great dream. On the other hand, through a new subjective approach to gaining knowledge, we had for the first time a reliable and systematic means to explore the finest levels of our consciousness.[74]

Six hundred studies from over 160 research institutions around the world have emerged from Wallace's pioneering work. The scientific research documenting the benefits of Transcendental Meditation are conveniently collated in a series of six volumes each the size of a telephone book and affectionately known as the Collected Papers.[75, 76]

Studies have shown not only that measurable physiological changes occur during Transcendental Meditation that set it apart from simply sitting resting,[77] but also that outside the meditation period people experience less anxiety,[78] a greater sense of well-being, greater self-actualisation,[79] they use their doctors and hospitals less often and enjoy better physical health.

In my own practice, as well as helping those with high blood pressure, I have helped patients with depression, migraine, dyspepsia, obesity and asthma to name just a few disorders, by recommending that they learn Transcendental Meditation. Transcendental Meditation has been used to rehabilitate Vietnam war veterans, help schoolchildren in their studies, help people recovering from alcoholism, keep airline pilots awake, and combat corporate stress. In business it has been used by such industry leaders as Siemens, and Sumitomo Heavy Industries, among countless others. In Senegal and many other parts of the world it has been used to rehabilitate thousands of prison inmates, while in a United States still coming to terms with the Colombine school disaster, schools are showing interest in learning more about how to decrease stress and violence using Maharishi's system of consciousness-based education. Millions of people from all parts of the world every day experience the feelings of happiness and ease of life that results when the mind learns how to transcend thought.

We can see from the scientific studies that Transcendental Meditation turns out to create both mental and physical health. Just as your body knows how to heal your finger when it is cut, without you having to get involved in the details, it seems that your body also knows how to become whole, once the mind leads the way by experiencing pure consciousness.

Earlier we implied that if we could create wholeness, then disease might fall away rather as shadows disappear when we turn on the light. We commented that this would stand orthodox medicine on its head, since medicine usually tries to eliminate disease in a piecemeal fashion. Or perhaps it is better to say that it would be like putting medicine up the right way again. Attending to diseases one by one is rather like watering the leaves and branches of an upside-down tree. Far better to attend to the root of the tree (as we show in Figure 3).

Some people cannot possibly imagine achieving the profoundly settled state of pure consciousness. They worry that their minds are so active that they will not be able to learn Transcendental Meditation successfully. It would be a lame technique if one had to be relaxed before one started though! As Maharishi says, if you can run you can walk. The ability to walk is inherent in the ability to run. If the mind is found to be running then it must be able to settle down and walk. If you can think, then you can transcend thought. You will find that the process is as natural to you as water running down a hill.

Much of the scientific work on Transcendental Meditation's effect on blood pressure has appeared in the context of stress research. The concept of stress, while less powerful in this regard than the idea of

Figure 3: Health Care All Upside Down

The human race is like a great uprooted tree, with its roots in the air. We must plant ourselves again in the universe.

—D. H. Lawrence

Water the root to enjoy the fruit.

—Maharishi Mahesh Yogi

Attending to diseases one by one is like watering the leaves and branches of an upside-down tree. We can create health more easily by attending to pure consciousness, the most fundamental field of life. Thereby we improve all aspects of the physiology, including blood pressure. Planted once again in the universe, we enjoy balance and wholeness of life.

pure consciousness, is, in a way, medicine's answer to reductivism. The term was coined by Dr Hans Selye, an eminent Canadian physician. Selye recounts as a young medical student, he watched a series of clinical case presentations. One by one the patients were wheeled in and described by the professor, each with a markedly different set of symptoms and different diagnosis. Yet Selye was struck by something the professor did not seem to mention or think important. Each patient, thought Selye, *looked sick*. Borrowing a term from engineering, Selye decided to call this common link between the patients 'stress'. He, and others since, have gone on to examine with great precision the biochemical and physiological characteristics of animals and human beings when under stress.[80] These changes Selye called the General Adaptation Syndrome.

In a profession lost among the small boundaries of reductivism, a terminology that could describe a common link among sick people was revolutionary. The word 'stress' (as applied to people) caught on in the public mind and quickly became part of our everyday language.

Selye described three stages of the General Adaptation Syndrome. The first, called the 'fight or flight' reaction, includes the acute production of adrenaline in the body with increased heart rate and a redistribution of blood flow to heart, brain and muscles. This is probably the state Cresswell Jones was in when presenting to his doctor at the beginning of this book. Blood pressure is very likely to be raised in this state. The second stage is the stage of resistance, in which the acute reactions described above decrease and the organism seems to have adapted successfully to the stressor. Blood pressure is raised in most subjects in this stage also. Any further stress during the second stage will be dealt with less successfully. The organism has lost adaptability. It is no longer 'light on its feet' and, if subjected repeatedly to chronic stress, it may lose its adaptive capability altogether and collapse into the third stage, which is exhaustion.

One person's stress trigger may be another's excitement, or opportunity. If two people are to take a bungy jump, one might react with fear whereas the other enjoys the 'buzz'. One of my patients confessed that, before learning Transcendental Meditation, he had regarded a red traffic light as a 'personal insult'. He now takes a red light as an opportunity to switch on the radio and listen to some music. Red lights remain red lights, but somehow he has turned what was a stressful phenomenon to his advantage.

The difficulty in 'standardising' people's reactions to stress made it difficult to define tightly the relationship between a stressor (a stressful life event) and stress (the subject's reaction to the event). We all react so differently. Thus the relationship of say, the loss of a spouse or loss of employment to sustained hypertension has been hard to pin down. Framingham data on men followed over a twenty-year period did show that middle-aged men with high levels of anxiety were at greater risk of subsequent hypertension, but this did not seem to apply to women.[81] Those reporting the data postulated that perhaps women have better 'social support mechanisms' that allow them to deal with their anxiety-provoking situations more easily.

Nevertheless, as we have seen, non-industrialised populations do not experience rising blood pressure as they grow older. The idea that this might be because they live less stressed and happier lives suggested another line of research. One very elegant study was carried out by researchers in Italy. For twenty years they followed 144 nuns who belonged to a secluded monastic order and compared their blood pressure to 138 of their peers who remained in society as householders. Whereas the laywomen's blood pressures rose over the years, the nuns' did not. The researchers concluded that 'the increase in blood pressure in women over twenty years may be avoided by living in a stress-free monastic environment characterised by silence, meditation and isolation from society'.[82]

It is not possible for most of us to insulate ourselves from society, yet it is not hard to imagine the effect our stressed, fragmented, society might have on our blood pressure. A recent study from the University of Michigan School of Public Health found a statistical link between feelings of hopelessness and hypertension.[83] The study of 616 middle-aged men showed that those who suffered from feelings of hopelessness (defined as a sense of futility and negative expectations about the future) were three times more likely to develop hypertension than men who did not suffer from these feelings. It is now increasingly recognised that anger is associated with hypertension also. While an individual may not appear overtly wrathful, he or she may be suppressing their frustration and rage, perhaps not even recognising it in themselves. It is well known that an outburst of fury can produce an acute elevation in blood pressure and it now seems probable that long-term inhibition of anger contributes to chronically elevated blood pressures.[84]

As we have mentioned, the currently favoured pathophysiological explanation for essential hypertension is that stress increases the activity of the sympathetic nervous system (the fight or flight reaction) which acts on the heart to increase cardiac output and on the arterioles to increase the peripheral resistance to the blood, as well as on the renin/angiotensin system. This causes the blood pressure to rise, at least in the early stages of hypertension. The body then somehow 'resets' itself at the higher level of blood pressure and the condition becomes self-perpetuating.

How can we reverse that situation? There are many 'stress management techniques' available that try to regain for us the stress-free life. Taken together and their results averaged out, they yield equivocal results on blood pressure, prompting one reviewer to conclude that they performed no better than placebo techniques.[85] Unfortunately this reviewer was performing meta-analysis in which the results of a great many stress-management techniques (including Transcendental Meditation) were lumped together and averaged. He had assumed that one stress-management technique is about as good as any other. This is misleading, since most of the techniques he was studying would have been the type of 'contemplation' or 'concentration' techniques that we have already sharply differentiated from Transcendental Meditation. Other analyses have found that Transcendental Meditation (endorsed by Selye himself in the later stages of his career) when considered in relation to other stress management techniques stands out above all others.[86]

Why does Transcendental Meditation turn out to be so effective in combating stress while other 'stress management' techniques are not? Here we must return to our consideration of pure consciousness. While Transcendental Meditation is indeed a very effective stress-management technique, as we have seen, this is not its primary purpose, nor is the conceptual framework upon which the term stress is based adequate to describe the full effects of Transcendental Meditation. As we have also seen, the purpose of Transcendental Meditation is to allow the subject to transcend the fragmented world of thoughts to experience, at the source of thought, the deep inner quiescence of pure consciousness. Whereas other techniques set out to create relaxation and lower stress levels, these are merely a by-product as far as Transcendental Meditation is concerned. The mind and the body are intimately connected and as we become familiar with the more integrated experience of pure consciousness the physiology begins to reflect that experience. It assumes a more integrated style of physical functioning, the parts of the body beginning to function more in accordance with each other. In short, the body becomes more healthy. This is such a genuine phenomenon that it can be demonstrated by standard physiological measurement. In creating health, stress simply falls away.

Apart from the comprehensive scientific research, perhaps the most compelling illustration of this ability of Transcendental Meditation to create health is its degree of professional medical acceptance. Thirty years of scientific research documenting its benefits have prompted thousands of doctors to practise Transcendental Meditation. Many more recommend Transcendental Meditation to their patients. In most countries groups of doctors have formed to promote the use of Transcendental Meditation in their professional lives and in those of their colleagues. In Holland since the late 1980s some insurance companies have been prepared to give substantial reductions in health insurance premiums (up to 40 percent in some instances) for people who practise Transcendental Meditation. In some parts of Britain, if a general practitioner prescribes Transcendental Meditation for a health reason, then the person can learn for free, under the National Health Service.

We began Part Three of this book in a 'quest for wholeness', having decided it was unsatisfactory to recommend treatment on a population basis unless it helped the person as a whole and therefore caused no harm. Drugs we found unacceptable as they help only one small part of the person, the part connected with the mechanical production of blood pressure. We found Transcendental Meditation to be a suitable candidate for our purposes, because it creates wholeness first, then brings blood pressure down as a consequence. In the next chapter we will examine more closely the scientific literature that documents the effect of Transcendental Meditation on blood pressure. In the meantime it looks as if Cresswell Jones is about to expand his horizons.

Jones is at the hardware store looking for fencing wire and strainer posts. You need something decent to keep a llama in. As he approaches the check-out counter he sees the familiar form, all 16 stone of it, of Michael O'Shaunessy ambling amiably towards him. O'Shaunessy has a good job with the City Council as a building inspector. Both men belong to Rotary and have chatted from time to time. O'Shaunessy has a wide circle of friends and lives well. He always looks happy, thinks Cresswell. Doesn't matter what's happening, he always has that big grin. Don't suppose he has high blood pressure. Too bad about the cough though. He should really give up those smokes. He needs to give up more than I do. 'Hey Cresswell,' says O'Shaunessy. 'I got just the thing for you! You're always stressed out. My wife's taking up this meditation! I've told her I'm going along too, just to keep her company. Besides, it's cheaper if we both do it together. Hey, why don't you come along? The talk's this Wednesday. There's nothing to lose!' Somewhere in the deep recesses of Cresswell's preconscious, a marble slowly rolls along its groove, gently nudges its neighbour which, in turn, causes a small light-bulb to illuminate dimly. Meditation! That word again! Only this morning Daphne mentioned it. Something about her friend saying it was cool. First Ellen, then Daphne and now Mike O'Shaunessy, of all people. 'How did you find out about it?' he asks. 'Aw, it's in the newspaper,' says Mike. 'Big article last Thursday. Lots of people do it. There's one or two football players and members of the cricket team . . .' 'Did you say football players? Really?' 'Yeah, and doctors and professors and all sorts.' Cresswell glances round the shop to make sure no one is in earshot. Everyone appears to be absorbed in their own business. 'All right Mike,' he says. 'You're on. But just out of interest.'

TEN

The Proof of the Pudding

Whether or not you are in line for a stroke, you can only benefit from practising Transcendental Meditation. For this reason, from a health authority's point of view, Transcendental Meditation, like advising people to stop smoking or to get more exercise, is an ideal population strategy. We have thus identified Transcendental Meditation as an intervention which fulfils our requirements in our plan to escape the epidemiologist's dilemma.

The randomised controlled trial (RCT), while telling us very little about individuals, can give us excellent information about populations. The RCT is the appropriate tool for assessing the results of a population strategy. Many studies that have researched the beneficial effects of Transcendental Meditation have used the randomised controlled design.

Such studies are difficult to organise, require expertise and time and are expensive. RCTs are commonly funded by pharmaceutical companies, because they are among the few organisations that can afford them. The other main avenues for funding are university, government or private grants. With commendable diligence and resolve, a group of scientists led by Dr Robert Schneider has been able to secure funding from the United States government to perform trials in which subjects randomly assigned Transcendental Meditation are compared with those randomly assigned to other 'stress management' techniques.

Dr Schneider's group has collaborated with other scientists working in the field of cardiovascular research and has been extremely active. Their results are exciting. Along with his colleague the late Dr Charles Alexander, Schneider studied the effects of Transcendental Meditation on hypertension in 127 African American men and women between the ages of 55 and 85 in Oakland, California. Subjects were randomly assigned to learn Transcendental Meditation, another relaxation technique known as progressive relaxation or to follow the usual kind of non-pharmacological advice that Cresswell Jones tried (and found wanting) earlier in this book. After three months, the Transcendental Meditation group, compared to the 'usual advice' group, lowered their systolic blood pressure by an average of 10.7 mm Hg ($p<0.0005$) and diastolic blood pressure by 6.4 mm Hg ($p<0.00005$)—to about the same degree as would be expected from a pharmaceutical drug. The progressive relaxation group showed lower blood pressures than the 'usual advice' group, but only about half as great as the meditating group (see Figure 4).[87]

> The significance of these studies cannot be over-emphasised. They show that Transcendental Meditation lowers blood pressure as reliably and as effectively as . . . antihypertensive drug therapy.

We saw earlier that doctors are now moving to identify subgroups in the hypertensive population who are at greater risk, smokers or diabetics, for example, and treat them preferentially. Could it be that Transcendental Meditation only helps lower blood pressure in some people, perhaps even those who are not at greater risk? To help answer this question, a further analysis of the data was carried out. Transcendental Meditation was found to be equally effective in reducing blood pressure in subjects with the highest risk profile for cardiovascular disease, including subjects with higher levels of smoking, drinking, obesity, salt intake, and low physical activity. The Transcendental Meditation group also showed improvements in how they perceived their health, social isolation and anger compared with other groups.[88]

Lower Blood Pressure

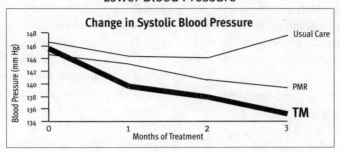

Figure 4: As Good as a Drug, only Better

Subjects randomly assigned to Transcendental Meditation, progressive relaxation or usual dietary and lifestyle advice were followed for three months. The Transcendental Meditation group showed a highly significant lowering of blood pressure, both systolic (shown here) and diastolic. The improvement in blood pressure with regular practise of Transcendental Meditation was found to be comparable to that seen with the use of drugs, but without harmful side-effects.

The significance of these studies cannot be over-emphasised. They show that Transcendental Meditation lowers blood pressure as reliably and as effectively as seen in the controlled trials of antihypertensive drug therapy. To fulfil our criteria for our first escape strategy from the 'drug bombing' mentality, we decided that we need an intervention that is as effective as drugs, cost-effective, safe and available. The efficacy of Transcendental Meditation has been demonstrated. The expenses involved in teaching Transcendental Meditation amount to a fraction of the cost of a lifetime of drug-taking and in addition it has wide-ranging health benefits for which there is a wealth of evidence, including studies that show directly that practitioners make less use of their medical services than non-practitioners.[89] Transcendental Meditation is therefore exceptionally cost-effective, and it is available in most cities of the world (see Useful Web-Pages, page 222). We find then that Transcendental Meditation fulfils our criteria, not just theoretically, but in the field as well. In the great majority of circumstances we do not need to use drugs. We have a proven alternative that not only brings your blood pressure down; it will make you feel better into the bargain.

Remember how few people actually ended up taking all their prescribed antihypertensive medication? By contrast, compliance with Transcendental Meditation in the above study was an impressive 97 percent. People look forward to their Transcendental Meditation sessions. Those who were lucky enough to be assigned to the

Transcendental Meditation group were enthusiastic. One subject reported: 'I always thought I was relaxing at home, but I just discovered there is an art to relaxing! It was fantastic! I felt all the

'That's my pill, and that's the best pill you can take.'

stress draining out of me.' All participants reported they prefer meditation to medication. The only complaint came from a woman who was irritated that her doctor hadn't told her about Transcendental Meditation. Her advice: 'Get your doctor to recommend Trans-cendental Meditation. That's my pill, and that's the best pill you can take.' When the programme ended, the participants got together by themselves and petitioned to have the study continued!

Dr Charles Alexander, a Harvard-trained psychologist who co-authored the study, commented: 'As a psychologist it was interesting to note the value that the people placed on practising their Trans-cendental Meditation technique. For this community, the Western medical model did not have very much impact. But they understood the value of this program, they realised how much it helped their lives.'

How does Transcendental Meditation lower blood pressure? If hypertension results from a stress-induced overstimulated sym-pathetic nervous system, then we might expect that Transcendental Meditation restores the sympathetic nervous system to a less agitated state. Recent work suggests that this is indeed the case. A lower sympathetic tone in turn relaxes the arterioles producing a lower peripheral resistance to the blood (in our analogy like taking one's finger off the nozzle of a hose), hence bringing blood pressure down. In a study of 32 healthy adults, 18 of whom were long-term practitioners of Transcendental Meditation, the non-meditators were asked to close their eyes and 'relax as completely as possible' for 20 minutes, while the meditators were asked to practise 20 minutes of meditation. The meditators showed an average drop of 3 mm Hg systolic blood pressure compared to a 2 mm Hg rise in the non-meditators. 'Total peripheral resistance'—a measure of the resistance to blood flow within the arterioles—decreased significantly in meditators, about 6.5 percent compared to a 1.6 percent rise in the attempting-to-relax non-meditators.[90]

Hypertension, as we have seen, is but a surrogate end-point for cardiovascular disease. If Transcendental Meditation can lower the blood pressure so effectively, and improve other risk factors besides,[91] could we expect to see fewer deaths from heart disease, and, indeed fewer deaths from any cause, if practitioners of Transcendental Meditation were followed over an extended period? Already Dr David Orme-Johnson had followed 2000 practitioners of Transcendental Meditation in Iowa over a five-year period and noted that the Transcendental Meditation practitioners used their health insurance policies, on average, about half as much as other health insurance customers. Whereas approximately 10 out of 1000 people not practising Transcendental Meditation made claims relating to heart disease, less than 2 per 1000 among the meditator group made such claims, a significant reduction, and indeed claims were fewer among all disease categories.[92] This was an observational study. Perhaps the subjects were 'self-selected', meaning that for some reason only people who are not going to get heart disease learn Transcendental Meditation. A study was needed in which subjects were randomly assigned either to Transcendental Meditation or another technique, and the subjects followed over a long period of time. This has now been done. Those practising Transcendental Meditation showed a significantly lower risk of death from both cardiovascular and any cause in an African American group followed for 5 years.[93] The relative risk reduction was about 68 percent. In a white population followed for 15 years, among those who died from heart disease, the mean survival time in the Transcendental Meditation group was significantly longer than in the other groups (11.4 years for the Transcendental Meditation group as compared to 9.91 years for the other groups).[94]

More reports of studies confirming the cardiovascular benefits of practising Transcendental Meditation are appearing rapidly in the world medical literature. From the University of Westminster in London comes the finding that Transcendental Meditation alleviates cardiac syndrome X. In cardiac syndrome X the subject experiences angina and performs poorly on exercise stress testing for angina (the 'treadmill' test). The symptoms may mimic unstable angina and lead to expensive investigations and hospital admissions. It also affects subjects' enjoyment of life, self-esteem and employment. In this pilot study, researchers found that regular practise of Transcendental Meditation dropped the frequency of angina episodes by more than 50 percent, the duration of the episodes decreased dramatically, and exercise performance improved significantly after just three months' practise of Transcendental Meditation.[95]

> A very exciting randomised clinical trial from Drew University in the United States ... suggests that simply practising Transcendental Meditation actually reverses atherosclerosis.

A very exciting randomised clinical trial from Drew University in the United States, recently published in the American Heart Association journal *Stroke*, suggests that simply practising Transcendental Meditation actually reverses atherosclerosis. Atherosclerosis is the narrowing of the arteries that we have seen is behind angina, heart attack and stroke.[96] Using ultrasound, the researchers were able to estimate very accurately the level of fatty substances deposited on the wall of study participants' carotid arteries by measuring the thickness of the lining of the artery (the intima-media thickness, or IMT). Sixty hypertensive African American subjects were randomly assigned to either Transcendental Meditation or a 'usual care' control group. The findings were impressive. After an average intervention period of seven months, those assigned to the Transcendental Meditation group showed a decrease of 0.098 mm in IMT (lining thickness) whereas the 'usual care' group showed an increase of 0.054 mm. These may not sound large differences, but based on previous studies these represent a significant reduction in risk of stroke. This is the first time that a mental technique has been shown to have a physical effect on the arteries.

Although concentrating mainly on heart disease, scientists at Dr Schneider's centre have also noticed improvements in other areas. One preliminary finding, that the death rate from cancer among meditators was about 50 percent less than the control groups, is being followed up with collaborators in Chicago. The ultimate goal of his centre, Dr Schneider said, was 'to create a disease-free society'. An ambitious aim? Perhaps not, when we remember that Transcendental Meditation creates health. Creating health, rather than fighting diseases, one by one, is an easier task.

Recently the group received a prestigious $8 million grant to establish a Center for Natural Medicine and Prevention. This will operate as a branch of the National Institutes of Health and has been selected as one of a number of centres of excellence for research in 'complementary' medical approaches around the United States.

Can we say, based on this work, that if one learns Transcendental Meditation one can be *guaranteed* never to have a heart attack? The answer must be no, for the reasons we outlined when we studied the limitations of epidemiological trials. Though your *risk* of a heart attack will be markedly lower, the possibility cannot be ruled out on the basis of these studies. These studies say that if you are like most people, you have about the same chance of lowering your blood pressure after three months with regular practise of Transcendental Meditation as you would if you took a pharmaceutical drug— but without the side-effects—and that consequently your *risk* of a heart attack will be very significantly lower. There is another big difference in favour of choosing Transcendental Meditation over drugs, though. If a drug does not work for you, it probably never will. You are among the 40 percent of 'non-responders'. By contrast, in my experience, nobody is a non-responder where Transcendental Meditation is concerned. Almost everyone receives benefit of one kind or another within the first few days, and the benefits are cumulative as time goes on. Because Transcendental Meditation is creating health on a broad front, then if it does not bring your blood pressure down immediately, the answer is 'keep creating health'! If your blood pressure does not respond immediately, this is because other areas of your life are being improved first. You may notice more energy at work or a better relationship with your children. It is in the nature of the process that is going on, that eventually your blood pressure will fall into line.

ELEVEN

Cresswell Makes His Move

Just before the introductory talk on Transcendental Meditation, Cresswell gets an attack of seriously cold feet. Just what is this thing he's getting into? Meditation? Does that mean beads? Sandals? Living in a cave? When Mike and Shirley turn up to take him to the talk he nearly pleads a headache. Still, Dr Feldstein hadn't rubbished the idea, once he had plucked up courage to ask him about it. 'Can't see how it could do you any harm, old boy,' had been his professional response, then he went on to say that it seemed to be good for some people, even one or two of his colleagues were doing. it. So if Feldstein was happy about it then maybe it was all right. 'You sure this is a good idea?' he asks Mike. 'Hey, you gotta come. I'm counting on you for moral support,' grunts the other genially. So they go. Shirley all buzzy and excited, Mike benign but wary and Cresswell frankly nervous. On entering the hall where the lecture is to be held, Cresswell finds, to his surprise, that there is not a bead or sandal in sight. Just a comfortably furnished lecture hall, a large vase of flowers tastefully arranged and an audience who look like the sort of people he works with most of the week. Decent hard-working citizens. A broad cross-section of young and old. He smiles and nods to a class-mate from his old school. He also identifies a well-known psychologist, a local sports identity, some older women who have obviously come to the talk together, a young man, possibly a university student, a rather bohemian-

looking tradesman in blue jeans, a group of white-collar workers and the managing director of a large retail outlet, one of his clients. A fresh-faced man, maybe forty, neatly attired, introduces himself as Aaron and begins by asking them how they found out about Transcendental Meditation and what attracted them to it. Many people in the audience know someone who does Transcendental Meditation already. Some have seen an item on TV. They have a variety of reasons for coming. The director is looking for a way to increase his efficiency and, like Cresswell, to bring his blood pressure down. The psychologist is hoping he might be able to reach out to his clients more effectively if his mind were clearer. The butcher's wife suffers from migraine headaches, and the older women are hoping to find something to help improve their memory and help them sleep more easily. The student wants to be able to concentrate better on his studies and the tradesman tells the group he is looking for inner peace and a greater sense of direction.

Aaron continues: 'Transcendental Meditation is a simple, natural technique that allows the mind to spontaneously experience progressively finer states of thought. The thinking process is then transcended altogether, and we are just left with ourselves, the Self, or as it is called, pure consciousness.'

Cresswell wonders what pure consciousness is, but decides the man will probably explain that in due course. He settles down to listen.

'When you begin Transcendental Meditation, you sit down, close the eyes and start a simple technique. Quite spontaneously, your mind starts to settle. As the mind settles, the body settles as well, and you become aware of a very deep state of rest. Research shows that while you are meditating the physiology changes profoundly in the direction of greater rest. Oxygen consumption falls, breathing slows and there is a reduction in the output of hormones such as the stress hormone cortisol and prolactin.

'You come out of meditation feeling refreshed and revitalised. The experience after meditation is very much like after sleep. You know how the day goes well after a good night's sleep? People get nicer, jobs get easier, the world is altogether a more benign and happy place. On the other hand, on a day after a bad night's sleep, without our having to think about it, problems abound. This is because rest is the basis of activity.'

Aaron continues with his talk and Cresswell likes what he hears. Aaron outlines the course of instruction, which involves another short talk, a personal interview, one-on-one personal instruction and four group classes each of one and a half hours, the first three being on the three days after personal instruction. Cresswell checks his diary and realises that with a little juggling he can make all the classes. This takes care of the first of the three requirements for the course. The next he has no trouble meeting, no marijuana for 15 days prior to the course, although he notices the tradesman enrols for a later course. His teacher explains that this requirement is a physiological matter, since marijuana and other non-prescribed drugs can leave a residue which interferes with the transcending process. Cresswell also discovers that Transcendental Meditation is taught by a non-profit educational organisation and that there is a financial investment required of him to begin the course. He reasons that they have to run the organisation somehow. There seems to be a lot of teacher input offered, and, as his teacher points out, once he has learned the technique the actual practice of it is free for the rest of his life. Cresswell reflects that it will be a worthwhile investment. Transcendental Meditation, it seems, will not only help bring his blood pressure down, it will help him gain peace of mind, clarity of thought, better ability to concentrate, relief from his insomnia and help him make more use of his latent abilities. Not bad if it can do all that! Cresswell decides to take the plunge. He books in for a course of instruction.

TWELVE

Your Best Medicine

Cresswell and Conventional Non-pharmacological Methods

Cresswell's course does not begin for another two weeks. Meanwhile, he wants to do everything he can to improve. Always a conscientious man, he has persisted among the unhappy ranks of those grimly pounding their way to better health. He returns from his evening run, grey and exhausted, and tells his wife, Ellen, how fit he is feeling. She tries not to remember the sad tale of her neighbour's doctor who had been an expert in sports medicine, until, at the age of 43, to everyone's surprise he had had a heart attack while on a run through the city park. Jones has cut out salt completely. Dinner now tastes bland and unappetising. He tells Ellen he prefers it that way. He has lost a little weight—a few pounds, but he was not greatly overweight in the first place. He has been told a glass of wine is good for his heart, but he has had a slight tendency to over-indulge in alcohol in the past, and he has heard that alcohol can damage the liver and put his blood pressure up. He has been told not to drink milk and to cut down on dairy products. But doesn't he need calcium for his bones? The advice he has been offered all seems very piecemeal and fragmented.

Diet and lifestyle play a large part in causing the major diseases of our society. Mr Jones is well motivated, yet he does not seem to be getting much joy from his attempts. What is going wrong?

Here we come to consider our second and third ploys for avoiding the tyranny of drug therapy. Our first was to continue the present medical strategy of making a 'blanket recommendation', but to make sure that our recommendation was to nobody's detriment. We identified Transcendental Meditation for that. In a sense already the job is done, we can lower blood pressure reliably. At least we know we can on a population basis, but what if you have learned Transcendental Meditation, you are sleeping better, your family life has improved, but your blood pressure has not yet improved? At the end of the last chapter we said 'keep creating health'. This is well and good, but is there not some way of making sure it happens more quickly for you? Remember that our second escape strategy was to give each person exactly the treatment that he or she needs to bring their blood pressure down. While Transcendental Meditation is working for us in the background, creating the integrated physiology that will be the ground for perfect blood pressure, maybe we can be doing something else in the meantime, something that is styled for each of us as a unique individual. This will involve diet and lifestyle, but not quite as Cresswell Jones has been approaching them.

In 1989 four men embarked from New Zealand's Auckland harbour bound for Fiji in a small trimaran, the *Rose-Noelle*. Most of them had very little experience of sailing and were relying on the long experience of their skipper. Three days out to sea they were caught in a fearful storm. Just when it seemed to have abated, the unthinkable happened. Their craft, normally known for its stability, capsized and they were left clinging to a wallowing, upside down, partially submerged hulk, in the wintry South Pacific Ocean. At night they huddled together in the one dry section remaining, a compartment 50 cm high and about the size of a double bed. Searchers eventually gave up all hope of finding them. What followed became one of the great stories of maritime survival. After drifting for 119 days, they came ashore on an outlying island known as Great Barrier Island from where they were eventually rescued. Their adventure had many unusual aspects, including the fact that, as the *Rose-Noelle* broke up on contact with the rocks of Great Barrier Island, they lost almost all evidence of their ordeal and the authorities at first refused to believe their story![97]

When four people were subjected to a radical change in diet and lifestyle, one got better and three got worse! What suits one person does not suit another.

Of interest here though is that while three of the men were in poorer condition, both mentally and physically, than they had been before the journey, suffering from constipation, loss of weight, and general debility, one of them, named Phil, seemed to thrive under the conditions. On leaving shore, he had been overweight, he had had a coronary artery bypass operation three years previously and was taking tablets to protect him from angina. While adrift, his diet consisted mainly of fish which they caught when they could and he frequently went hungry. He lost weight. Smoking was out of the question. He also got a fair amount of exercise one way or another, squeezing through the small hole they had made in the hull of the boat, and attempting to catch fish with a gaff. He completely forgot to take his angina tablets. At the end of their adventure he was lean and trim and told his rescuers that he felt better than he had ever felt in his life!

When four people were subjected to a radical change in diet and lifestyle, one got better and three got worse! What suits one person does not suit another. Unfortunately this is not taken into account when official recommendations for diet and lifestyle are given. Non-pharmacological approaches have been evaluated with the same mind-set that we use to evaluate drugs. The idiosyncracies that make each one of us special tend to be left out of the equation. As far as his lifestyle is concerned, Cresswell Jones is still caught in the epidemiologists' dilemma. He will be lucky if following the conventional non-pharmacological guidelines allows his escape!

It is commonly held that a moderate amount of exercise (say 20 minutes of brisk walking, or running, three times a week) is beneficial for blood pressure.[98] In most cases this is probably true. However, we are again talking here about 'Mr Average'. Jogging is an excellent activity for some. It suits some people. It does not seem to suit Mr Jones. The Australian Aborigines, who in their pre-European state enjoyed extremely low blood pressures and almost non-existent rates of cardiac disease, 'avoided physical activity not considered essential to their lifestyle, and today regard pointless activity like "jogging" with great amusement.'[8]

As we have seen, heart disease and stroke are virtually absent among the hunter-gatherer type of societies that continue to exist. In these cultures, hypertension is unknown. Yet when their members come to live in Western society, they quickly take on Western diseases. Similarly Phil started smoking and eating fatty meals almost immediately on reaching dry land and his angina came back. On the other hand, Aborigines who revert to their hunter-gatherer lifestyles have been shown, after three to six months, to reverse many of their health problems.

What is it about these peoples' lifestyle that makes them so healthy? Exercise, the absence of stress and diet all seem to play a part. In the dietary arena, one of the major suspects is sodium chloride, or common salt. In bygone times, salt was an expensive luxury. So highly was it prized that it was a form of currency. People were paid wages in salt, hence the phrase 'to be worth one's salt'. With improved methods of production and transport, Western societies can enjoy salt in an abundance never before possible. And enjoy it we do. Most of us take in at least 200 mmol of sodium per day, whereas rural tribesmen in Kenya would take only about 60–70 mmol per day. When the Kenyans move to Nairobi and adopt a more typically Western diet their salt intake increases and the average blood pressure for the population rises. Indigenous populations such as the Aborigines or the New Zealand Maori who have adopted the Western way of life show very high rates of hypertension, diabetes, obesity and cardiovascular disease.

That salt might be 'the culprit' in hypertension received major support from a massive worldwide study involving 10,079 men and women from 52 different populations, aged 20 to 59 years. Known as the Intersalt study, it was reported in 1988 to show a highly significant positive relation between 24-hour urinary sodium excretion (a measure of how much the kidneys are 'spilling' excess salt) and systolic blood pressure. The authors of the Intersalt report conclude that a sodium intake lowered by 100 mmol/ day—for example 70 instead of 170 mmol/day—could result in adults aged between 25 and 55 having a systolic blood pressure reduction of 10 mm Hg. They point out that this could 'substantially reduce rates of major cardiovascular diseases and mortality from all causes'. Their recommendation is that we should all reduce our intake of salt.[99]

'The Food Industry Fights for Salt'

Not everybody wants us to reduce our salt intake, most notably the food industry. Salt sells food. A reduction to below 100 mmol/day by everyone in Britain, for example, would cost the industry literally billions of pounds. In 1996, the *British Medical Journal* ran an editorial entitled 'The food industry fights for salt'. 'Like any group with vested interests, the food industry resists regulation. Faced with . . . the fact that most dietary salt (65–85 percent) comes from processed foods, some of the world's major food manufacturers have adopted desperate measures to try to stop governments from recommending salt reduction. Rather than reformulate their products, manufacturers have lobbied governments, refused to co-operate with expert working parties, encouraged misinformation campaigns, and tried to discredit the evidence.' This was, said the writer, 'the latest volley in a 20-year campaign by the food industry, waged since the role of diet in heart disease first became a public health issue.'[100]

The Intersalt study was of cross-sectional design, meaning that a 'snapshot' was taken of each population's average blood pressure and salt intake. Because it did not investigate the effect of changing salt intake over time, it can be criticised on theoretical grounds. Nevertheless it is compelling evidence and it seems very likely that if we could all eat less salt on average, then our average blood pressure would fall.

But do we all need to do that? The people of Akita in Northern Honshu, in Japan, have a diet mostly made up of miso soup, rice and pickles. Their salt intake has been enormous. As you might expect, they had a very high incidence of hypertension and a devastatingly high number of strokes. According to one authority, 'Forty percent of the population over 40 were hypertensive and the death rate from cerebral haemorrhage in people in their 50s was up to 4–8 times higher than for people in the USA, Britain and West Germany . . . 10 percent of the 55–59 age group had been paralysed by stroke.[8]

Public health measures have reduced the average daily intake of salt in Akita since 1969, and the prevalence of hypertension has declined. This seems to

. . . for some people, reducing salt intake actually raises blood pressure!

confirm our suspicions about the adverse effects of salt. However, the story continues: 'One signal fact in relation to the Japanese of Akita . . . is that whereas 40 percent of the population was hypertensive, 60 percent were not. An intake [of salt] 50 times higher than the preliterate populations was handled without BP increase.' So the majority of the Akita people were not affected by their massive salt intake at all. Furthermore, studies elsewhere have shown that, for some people, reducing salt intake *actually raises blood pressure!*[101]

We are caught again in our epidemiologist's dilemma. Data from populations cannot be applied to individual people. What is true for a population at large may not be true for Cresswell Jones, or you, or me. Doctors and policymakers, from their positions of authority, tell us to 'play it safe'. Adopt a bland and unappetising salt-free diet, they say. The food industry tells us we may not need to, so don't. Clearly some of us should reduce our salt intake, so the industry is not being entirely responsible. But which of us should follow what advice?

As we implied in Chapters Four and Five, our tendency to treat everyone with hypertension in the same way stems from an entrenched tendency within medicine to treat disease, rather than people. We try to 'hit' the disease with our 'bullets' or our blanket recommendations. Disease has become a 'thing', something that has an independent existence, independent of people, even. We can credit our mass acceptance of this notion to the great physician Thomas Sydenham who in 1676 proposed that 'Nature, in the production of disease, is uniform and consistent; . . . and the self-same phenomena that you would observe in the sickness of a Socrates you would observe in the sickness of a simpleton'.

There is another way to go about it though, and that is to treat *people*. Those who like to treat people feel that each person is unique and special. Therefore they do not 'name' very readily. They recognise that everyone's condition is different, that in fact, no two people have, for example, pneumonia or hypertension in quite the same way. These doctors appreciate deeply the different facets of a person's unique way of life. They see diversity but they do not try to categorise it. They revel in it. They build up a detailed picture of the individual, accepting differences, and people, for what they are. They do not try to categorise detail; they see it in relation to the whole. Like an artist minutely observing nature, yet creating a cohesive work of art, they use their knowledge of detail to promote harmony and balance in the patient. They see disease as an imbalance, a loss of wholeness. Where their counterparts saw 'disease in Man' they see 'Man in disease'.

Are You a Coan or a Cnidian?

Although 'holistic medicine' may seem a relative newcomer on the medical scene, the whole-picture, people-oriented approach dates at least to the Greeks, having its roots in the Coan school of thought, from the Isle of Cos, which in the Hellenistic Age of Ancient Greece was a favourite abode of men of letters. It was the birthplace of Hippocrates, and the centre of the medical school with which he is associated. The disease-centred approach, a rival school, was the school of Cnidus (Cnid is pronounced Nid, to rhyme with lid or skid) and this gave rise to the Cnidian approach.[102]

Here are some features that I associate with the Coan and Cnidian schools:

Coan and Cnidian characteristics compared

COANS	CNIDIANS
'Right brain'	'Left brain'
Tend to be intuitive	Tend to be cerebral
Subjective	Objective
Interested in people primarily	Interested in ideas, concepts, primarily
Fascinated by the 'thing in itself'	Like to categorise things and move on
Promote the individual	Promote law and order
Communicate with difficulty	Communicate easily and with authority
Humane outlook	Can be cold and 'clinical'

Associated with wholeness. Parts seen as contributing to the whole	Associated with fragmentation, reductivism
Nominalist. Believe that disease names are just shorthand conveniences	Realist—in the philosophical sense—believe that disease names refer to real entities
Hands on. Direct contact through history and examination	Indirect contact by measurement and statistics, population surveys
Have time to appreciate detail	Often in a hurry
Can seem to be woolly and inefficient, but think and feel deeply	Efficient. Get things done. Not much time for reflection
Know intuitively where they are going	More interested in getting there

While almost all doctors would imagine themselves to be 'patient-centred' and recognise it as a medical ideal, in reality most show a strong bias towards disease-centredness. We like to categorise the patient's illness and move on. Our hospital wards are organised according to disease types (respiratory wards, oncology wards) whereas it would be quite possible to arrange them according to people types. Whether sides of the brain have anything to do with it I am unsure, but the Cnidian approach does seem to conform to the qualities that many people have described as classically left brain, whereas the Coans seem to express the intuitive and artistic qualities ascribed to the right brain. Coan doctors like to spend time in getting to know the patient and appreciate the subtle details that make that person special.

Cnidians All

The bias towards Cnidus is not altogether the fault of the medical profession because in fact we are a society of Cnidians. As a group we like to measure, classify and pigeon-hole. The desolate sense of hopelessness, loneliness and loss of place that is so often associated with the twentieth-century Western community could be traced to this splintered style of thinking. As individuals we have become lost to ourselves and lost to our life-supporting links with others. In a society which has lost its unity, lost its soul, a return to the Coan path is urgently required.

While lesser physicians mostly seem to wander down the Cnidian track, paying lip-service to the Coans, the greatest physicians seem to combine the two approaches without degrading either. When Hippocrates says that he frames his judgements (or diagnoses) by paying attention to what was common to every, and particular to each case, he seems to be expressing both the Coan and Cnidian approaches simultaneously.

The word 'diagnosis' is made up of *gnosis*, meaning knowledge, and *dia*, which can mean through, but in ancient times probably meant *thorough* as in the word *diagram*, a thorough picture. *Diagnosis* means, or should mean, thorough knowledge. A Coan diagnosis implies thorough knowledge—the kind of picture a general practitioner might build up from years of contact with a patient through childhood, adolescence and parenthood, in their homes and in their relationships. Coan diagnoses are inclusive and intuitive, rich in feelings, insights and understandings. Coan diagnoses arise deep in the heart and soul of the physician. They are all to do with the patient as a whole. It can be difficult to put such a diagnosis into the boundaries of words. A Coan diagnosis may be difficult to communicate to another person, particularly someone of the Cnidian bent.[103]

As a Coan, Hippocrates was superb. Hippocrates liked to notice about each single patient 'the habits of life and occupation; to speech, conduct, silences, thoughts, sleep, wakefulness and dreams—their content and incidence; pickings and scratchings, tears, stools, urine, spit, and vomit; earlier and later forms of illness during the same prevalence; to critical or fatal determinations; to sweat, chill, rigor, hiccup, sneezing, breathing, belching, to passage of wind, silently or with noise; to bleedings; and to piles.' Hippocrates would not have been content with a five-minute blood pressure check!

Nor, indeed, should a sound present-day doctor. Unfortunately, though, while every medical student is taught the value of a human-istic approach, I have found that it remains an undeveloped art. Rather than notice what is particular about each, doctors tend to focus on what is common to every case. Groups of symptoms form a syndrome and a sufficiently well-established syndrome qualifies as a disease. This simplifies diagnosis, which now reduces itself to recognising a cluster of symptoms and matching this cluster to the appropriate disease label. Treatment is simple too, since each label has associated with it a standardised treatment regime, usually a drug. As long as you know he has asthma you don't really need to know the patient very well at all! Thus doctors can say things like: 'Come and see this very interesting liver in Ward 3!' or: 'Who is that old stroke in the corner?'

In the Cnidian model of medicine a disease is thought of as something apart from the patient. It is a thing, an entity which has a kind of independent existence of its own. We express this idea when we say someone has 'got pneumonia', as if the disease itself has jumped off one person and landed on another. This seems very logical in the case of pneumonia, since we all know about bacteria and viruses, and we know that they can indeed jump from one person to another. But is the germ the same thing as pneumonia? Doesn't getting pneumonia also depend on how your body reacts to that germ? You can have the germ and not have pneumonia. Plenty of people are exposed to the pneumococcus bacterium, but they do not get sick.

The germ theory of infectious diseases gave tremendous impetus to the Cnidian school, because it seems to support the idea of 'disease as thing'. In practice, we treat pneumonia, rather than people. So successful has it been that the disease model of medicine has become contagious in itself, spreading into areas of medicine in which it does not really sit well, areas which would be much better dealt with in a Coan kind of way. This is precisely what happened when we discovered that we could measure the pressure of the blood.

When we accept that disease is an 'entity' rather than an imbalance, faulty process, or loss of harmony within a unique individual, then it becomes very easy for that entity to acquire a kind of dark life of its own. We saw this in an earlier chapter in which the dog, hypertension, got away. This is why in ancient times diseases were identified with demons. A certain destiny or future, which doctors call the 'natural history of a disease', the course which a disease category has been observed in most cases to follow, is laid out and it has a kind of grim inevitability about it. If it can be supported by accurate statistics then it becomes all the more compelling. If we are not careful the natural history of a disease can become a self-fulfilling prophecy, a kind of modern-day 'pointing the bone'.

A 30-year-old man with a systolic blood pressure of 165 has

hypertension. When told that he has a 10 percent chance of having a heart attack or stroke by the age of 50, does it mean that he, personally, has just this chance? Of course not. That figure applies collectively to the particular group of people that was measured. It has been assumed that he is similar to them. It might not be true. He might have other completely unknown factors that make him special, that protect him from heart disease or stroke, or he might choose to live in a very healthy way, just as a very careful driver can beat the odds and avoid a motor vehicle accident. Because of these his chances might be 1 percent. As the Coans knew, we are all different. Furthermore, if we know how, we can *make* ourselves different, and beat the odds.

> ... the natural history of a disease can become a self-fulfilling prophecy, a kind of modern-day 'pointing the bone'.

Even in very serious illnesses in which the 'natural history' is certain death, there are recorded instances of spontaneous remission. The great aviator, sailor and adventurer Sir Frances Chichester accomplished his sailing feats with a diagnosis of advanced lung cancer. (He learned about his disease from a surgeon who, at the time, was exhibiting him to a group of medical students, an incident which left him feeling 'degraded, defiled and deeply depressed'.) With determination, the help of a healthy diet, a supportive wife, and an inspired French doctor, he recovered and proceeded to win the gruelling first solo Trans-Atlantic yacht race, eight days ahead of his closest competitor, among many other sailing feats.[104]

No Loss for Words

Cnidians have no trouble communicating their diagnoses accurately and authoritatively because diseases can be tightly defined. Disease categories can be easily expressed in words. Communication among Cnidian colleagues is quick and accurate, as is diagnosis and treatment. The current trend towards 'medical consultation software', which promises to give a diagnosis and treatment on input of the presenting symptoms, is a very Cnidian idea, as are the proliferating sets of 'medical guidelines', which appear designed to programme doctors to act in the same way for every patient who has the same disease, just as their computers do.

Its concepts being clear and easily expressed perhaps explain why the Cnidian school has gained almost complete authority in modern medicine. Only when ill-defined diagnoses such as hypertension refuse to respond to the Cnidian approach do the pitfalls in a purely Cnidian method become clear. For all the success of the Cnidian approach, no disease has any life outside of the particular human being who has it. That human being is unique and special and so, therefore, is the disease.

A good Coan might tell us what the population-based studies cannot. What sort of person have we here? Should this person cut back on salt, or is he among the group who needs it? Is she likely to respond to a low-fat diet, or will it even be harmful for her?

> Your blood pressure changes beat by beat. The wonderful thing about this is that you have the chance, every second of the day, to bring your blood pressure down!

When we (as Cnidians) say someone has cancer it sounds as if a rock has entered their body, even though cancer is still made of living (if confused) cells. Cancer cells change, they die and sometimes transmute. Pneumonia is not a static thing, it progresses. Your body is changing minute by minute. The Greek philosopher Plutarch said (quoting Heraclitus), 'We do not dip twice into the same wave, nor can we touch twice the same mortal being.' This is literally true, since in the short time it takes to touch someone twice, the molecules that compose that person have changed. For example, the person has breathed out carbon dioxide and breathed in oxygen molecules.

'All things fleet away,' said Heraclitus. Nowhere is this idea better exemplified than in hypertension. Your heart beats. About 70 ml of blood 'fleets away' into the circulation under a certain pressure. The next time it beats, less than a second later, the blood fleets under a different pressure. Maybe you have sat up. Or got angry. Perhaps you have started your evening Transcendental Meditation session. Your blood pressure changes beat by beat. The wonderful thing about this is that you have the chance, every second of the day, to bring your blood pressure down! What seemed like a 'disease' with all the grim inevitability that the word implies becomes something much more malleable.

Your Cnidian doctor may decide you have 'got' hypertension. A Coan doctor will take a different tack. She will ask herself, 'Why is this particular abnormality occurring in this particular patient at this particular time?' The one sees a malign entity with a dark agenda of its own. The other sees no such entity, just a human being whose changing body is behaving in a confused way. It is behaving in a way that is not in accordance with the whole. Since the body is changing anyway, then why not help it to change for the better?

Maharishi's Vedic Approach to Health includes a comprehensive diagnostic system to determine the patient's individual profile and the degree to which the body is in balance, or behaving in a confused way. The following anecdote illustrates how effectively this diagnostic system works.

Some years ago a young woman representing a pharmaceutical firm appeared in my surgery to try to interest me in a new drug for the treatment of dyspepsia. She held in front of me, along with a number of superbly presented graphs and displays, a glossy photograph depicting a group of six rather glum-looking people. The caption read: *These patients are suffering from the pain and discomfort of dyspepsia.* After studying the image for a minute I said, 'I can see only one person here who could definitely have dyspepsia. The rest look very unlikely candidates. How many of these people are real patients, and how many are models for the photographer?' The young lady seemed surprised. 'Which one do you think is real?' she said. 'This one,' I replied, pointing to a fair-skinned, dour-looking man of medium build. The woman now looked dumbfounded. 'Well yes,' she said. 'He has dyspepsia very badly. Actually these people are the staff of our head office. They were all called in for the photograph. I don't know of anyone else in the office who really has any symptoms. But that's amazing! How on earth did you know that!'

I leaned back luxuriously in my armchair, fingertips together. 'Quite simple, really, Watson,' I said, languidly.

Actually it *was* quite elementary. Dyspepsia is a cardinal symptom of what in Maharishi's Vedic Approach to Health is called a Pitta imbalance. Pitta is one member of what are known as the three doshas. The doshas can be regarded as physiological patterns of functioning. The other two doshas are called Vata, and Kapha. Vata is the principle that is associated with movement, Pitta is associated with energy and Kapha is associated with structure.

Only one of the six people in the photograph looked unequivocally Pitta-imbalanced. His reddish hair, medium build, fair and freckled complexion and such sourness of expression that it could not have been assumed, gave him away! Of the others, I thought two probably had the Pitta dosha present to a degree, but I did not think that it was likely to be in such excess as to cause symptoms. The remaining two were large, well-built people who represented much more strongly the Kapha pattern.

Each of the six billion people alive in the world today represents a unique interplay between these three basic elements, Vata, Pitta and Kapha. By understanding how the three doshas interact in the patient before us, we can understand that person as a special individual. We can know a lot about people by considering the three doshas. We now know why Jack Spratt had different tastes from his wife, for example.

As we saw, orthodox medicine tries to think of each person as being much the same as everyone else. In our 'best evidence' randomised controlled trials, we try to smooth out the differences between us all, by a process of averaging the measurements we make on large numbers of people. We could think of this as 'one person' medicine, in which we create the 'standard human being'. The 'standard human being' is rather like the 'standard milk' that we buy in our supermarkets; that is, milk that comes from so many thousands of different cows that each day differences average out and today's milk comes out as being pretty much the same as yesterday's. As we implied in our previous discussions, once you have your standard human being then you can measure the effects of standard drugs against standardised (Cnidian-based) diseases.

A randomised trial looking, for example, at the effect of a drug on hypertension does tell us some useful things. It tells us:

1. What happens to the average blood pressure in the treated population.

2. What *chance* exists that a given individual will experience a similar change in blood pressure, *if he is not too significantly different from the 'average person' in the study*.

Of course, we know from our knowledge of Maharishi's Vedic Approach to Health, that if all the people in the intervention group happened to be predominantly Kapha in type and all those in the 'dummy intervention' group happened to be Vata, and our patient happens to be Pitta, then the trial may not tell us as much as we hoped!

Leaving this aside and assuming that a good mix of the doshas was present in all populations, then it can be worthwhile to know that an intervention works more often than not for most people. For example, it helps screen out far-fetched ideas for therapy that have no value at all or may even be detrimental or dangerous. That other people have benefited from a treatment in say, 60 percent of cases, and that this has been studied in a formal way, establishes the credentials of a new therapy and gives us confidence to put a patient to the time and trouble of trying the treatment for him or herself. It is useful knowledge, provided we do not make interpretations from it that are unwarranted.

People often assume though that the randomised controlled trial gives us the ultimate answer on whether a drug or some other kind of intervention 'works'. If they wish to answer the question, does the drug enalapril 'work' or does restricting salt 'work' in treating hypertension, they scan the literature for randomised controlled trials.

What they forget to ask is 'work for whom?' This is a question that the trial cannot answer on a person-to-person basis. It can only say whether it 'works for most', or 'works for some'. The fact is that most people are significantly different from 'Mr Average'. Many doctors have recognised this fundamental limitation of multi-patient studies, the difficulty that exists in extrapolating from the study findings to individual patients. When you try a new treatment, say a drug, no matter how widely tested this has been on large populations, no one can say from the studies whether it will work for you. As mentioned previously, you may fall into the group of responders (usually no more than 60 percent for most antihypertensives) or you may be one of the 'non-responders', a full 40 percent of those who try the drug. As some researchers have pointed out, this means that every time a doctor prescribes a new drug for a patient, he is carrying out a small experiment.

Some have tried to formalise the experiment (with the patient's consent) by randomly substituting a 'dummy' drug in a patient's pill tray with neither doctor nor patient knowing whether the active or 'dummy' drug is being taken, and an independent experimenter assessing the patient's response to both dummy and active drug (these are called 'N of 1' studies).[105] In everyday practice, very few people carry out N of 1 studies, even though they are an intriguing methodology. Being too time-consuming to consider in a busy medical setting they have remained something of a research curiosity. In millions of doctors' surgeries all over the world, therefore, deciding whether a therapy 'works' for Joe Brown or Cresswell Jones is made entirely on an ad hoc, 'seat of the pants' basis. No one knows whether it will work until you try it. In the final analysis, the proof of the pudding is indeed in the eating.

Western medicine has made some attempt to allow for individual differences in predicting the likely response to an intervention. The early classification of people into endomorphs, mesomorphs and ectomorphs is an example, and in more recent times there has been an attempt to group people into type A or type B personality types, the type A being said to be more vulnerable to heart disease. More recently, there has been a move towards identifying the 'absolute risk' of cardiovascular disease in a given individual by considering not just one or two risk factors, but the combination of many risk factors taken together, such as previous heart attack, age, gender, diabetes, smoking, blood pressure, family history and blood cholesterol concentration. This is an attempt to build up a 'profile' of the individual patient. It is an essentially Cnidian attempt however, since it can only ever differentiate between subjects according to arbitrary subgroups, such as smoker/non-smoker, hypertensive/non-hypertensive. We might say it is the Cnidian school trying to be more Coan. If in this way we differentiate between, say, male and female, we are practising two-people medicine. Or we might consider separately young and old, or diabetics and non-diabetics, smoker and non-smoker and so forth and, with permutations and combinations perhaps get up to five, twenty or even a hundred 'people types'.

How many 'people types' are there? With about 6 billion people in the world it is safe to say, such is the incredible complexity of the genetic code, that no one person is identical to another. Even 'identical' twins are instantly recognisable from each other to those who know them. So does that mean there are 6 billion 'people types'? What about all the people that have ever lived? They were all different too. Those who are yet to live? The theoretical number of 'people types' is infinite. It is not surprising that predictions about drug effects based on the concept of the 'standard human being' sometimes go awry!

The three doshas are not arbitrary subgroups. They are fundamental principles deeply embedded in our nature. So perfectly do they describe us that we can use them to precisely characterise any human being who presents to us. A doctor or consultant proficient in Maharishi's Vedic Approach to Health understands each person as unique and builds a picture in his or her mind. Western medicine could not hope to emulate the refinement to which Maharishi's Vedic Approach to Health is able to differentiate between people.

The consultant will often have begun to frame his diagnosis— meaning not just a label, but *thorough knowledge* about the patient, before the patient has even sat down at the consultation desk. He will not be thinking of the patient as a 'standard human being'. The first glance at the patient's build, perhaps their demeanour and gait as they come through the door, will have already begun to suggest in the consultant's mind, the balance and imbalance of the doshas present, the nature of the person he will be treating and the likely symptoms of which the patient will complain. As he works with the patient he will continue to build on and refine this knowledge.

But Isn't This All in Our Genes?

When many doctors (and patients) begin to think about the differences between people and why it is that one person has hypertension and another does not, or perhaps why one person has a heart attack where another does not, their minds tend to drift towards the field of genetics. Often they stop there. We are different because of our genes. We can't do anything about our genes, so looking at the differences between people is a dead end. There is no point in being Coans. Let's go back to being Cnidians. This is the attitude my patient Sam was expressing.

About 15 years ago, Sam, a fit young man aged 20, consulted me for a trivial complaint which might have been a mild sore throat or something like that. In the course of my examination I measured his blood pressure and found it was higher than the WHO-defined normal value at that time. It should have been no higher than 140/90, whereas Sam's blood pressure was 160/100. Over the course of the next few weeks we took a number of measurements and each time we came up with a high reading. Sam appeared to have mild hypertension, or to be Coan about it, an imbalance existed in Sam's physiology. I cautiously began to acquaint Sam with some of the ideas I present in this book. I told him he would need to do something, but he did not necessarily need to go on drugs. Sam's reaction took me aback. 'It's OK doc,' he said with a resigned smile. 'My mother has had high blood pressure for years. She's been on pills for ages and they don't seem to have done her any harm. I didn't think I was likely to escape. So just give me the pills, and I'll be happy with that!' Nothing I could say would convince Sam otherwise, and eventually I gave in. Against my better judgement, I prescribed him a diuretic. Sam went away happy. The next time he came his blood pressure was normal, and it remained so for the next four years, Sam seeing me every three months for his blood pressure check and prescription.

Having lived a sedentary life as an office worker, Sam then rather suddenly became interested in the great outdoors. It became very important to him to have a clean bill of health so that he could take part in an outdoor training course designed to extend young men and women to the limits of their physical endurance. In preparation, Sam was cycling, tramping and generally becoming very physically fit. When he came to ask me if I would sign a medical certificate, he expressed concern that the presence of the diuretics might count against him in his acceptance on the course.

I suggested he stop them. We checked his blood pressure on a number of subsequent visits. It has remained completely normal and the long and short of it is that he has not required diuretics or any other drug for the last eleven years.

Sam obviously brought himself back into balance by a healthy dose of exercise. He probably also lost a little weight and quite probably improved his diet. But what about those genes from his mum? Surely hypertension is hereditary?

Medical researchers have long been aware that hypertension tends to cluster in families. So genetics plays a part. But it is only one factor among many. We tend to think, as Sam did, that what is in our genes is fixed. This leads to a kind of fatalism in which we feel we are doomed to whatever characteristics our genes dictate. There are some diseases that are said to be 'monogenic', in which one gene can be held responsible for the disorder. However, these diseases are mostly very rare, and the vast majority of disorders are 'polygenic', meaning that many genes act together to create the disorder.

Furthermore, while classical genetics assumes that genes are the basic elements that define the human body, this is a reductivist assumption that rests on the idea that our world is primarily made of little bits of matter. This is not necessarily so. It conflicts, for example, with the findings of quantum physics that holds that our world consists primarily of fields. There could be other more basic patterns of intelligence within these fields of which genes are simply an expression. These patterns could influence the 'playing out' of the genetic code.

An analogy may make this clearer. While it is true that all piano music consists of combinations of the notes represented by the black and white keys, it does not follow that knowing the sequence of black and white keys as they appear on a piano keyboard will yield the structure of a Bach fugue, even though the keys are laid out in a definite sequence from low to high notes. The genetic sequence may be rather like the black and white keys, rather than the fugue itself. The fugue requires a level of intelligence that transcends the sequence of the keys, in this case, the special input of the composer. In the same way, the sequence of genetic material in the DNA may be only part of the story in creating, for example, a human being. Although capable of carrying out a great deal of cellular 'housework', DNA may ultimately need to be informed by a level of intelligence that transcends it. This is certainly the view from Vedic Science, and would seem to be echoed by our 'theories of wholeness', in which 'higher-level ordering' is identified.

When you add to this the understanding that all genes interact with their environment, and that this affects the 'penetrance' of the gene (penetrance is the degree to which the gene expresses its characteristics into the environment) then we see that our genetic expression is not as fixed and deterministic as we might have thought. Geneticists now talk of the 'fluid genome' to express the fact that there is a constant interplay between each gene and the millions of other genes in the organism, and between them and the constantly changing internal and external environment. This is why, for example, genetically modified cotton crops have failed in certain weather conditions—the full effect of the environment was not predicted by the arrangement of genes in the plant's genome. Genetics, for all its complexity, remains a partial knowledge.

What this all adds up to is that if you have a strong family history of hypertension or of heart disease, it means you may be disposed towards these conditions, but it does not necessarily mean you are fated to contract them. I am not saying here that you can afford to be complacent. None of us can, and in fact you less than others. What I am saying is that you have to be even more alert to optimise as many of the other causative factors as possible. Genetic theory does not mean we should give up our quest to become Coans; rather, we should intensify that quest to discover as much as possible about ourselves.

Our consultant in Maharishi's Vedic Approach to Health automatically takes into account the environment in assessing the patient. As the patient walks into the consulting room, the consultant is aware of the weather outside, the time of day and the time of year. These environmental factors are all associated with the three doshas, and will, in turn, be influencing the pattern of the doshas in that particular patient in ways that the consultant can predict.

The Doshas Explained

Where are the three doshas, then? Do they live in the body, or in the world as a whole? What exactly are they? Are they material? According to Vedic Science the doshas are expressed at all levels of the universe, including our minds, thoughts, emotions, bodies and physical environment, but their home is actually hidden deep within the structure of the universe, at its very basis. Whereas, for mainstream Western thought, at least until the end of the nineteenth century, the basis of the universe was matter, in Vedic Science, the primary stuff of creation is not matter at all, but consciousness. Like currents forming ripples on the surface of a lake, the doshas are like interweaving patterns living and moving within the ocean of consciousness.

What is consciousness? When you are awake you are conscious. When you are asleep you are (generally) not. So consciousness is the quality of awakeness or lively alertness. This can be referred to as the quality of knowingness, self-knowing or self-referral. In the West, consciousness is generally regarded as an 'epiphenomenon', a kind of by-product of the complexity of the human brain. In the Vedic approach, it is seen the other way around. The human brain and indeed, the entire panoply of forms and phenomena that make up our universe, are expressions of consciousness.

That consciousness is primary may seem to be a surprising, even shocking idea. It may help to reflect that this conclusion has been arrived at by the more thoughtful among the Western physicists. Sir James Jeans expressed the idea when he said:

> Today there is a wide measure of agreement, which on the physical side of science approaches almost to unanimity, that the stream of knowledge is heading toward a non-mechanical reality; the universe begins to look more like a great thought than a great machine.[106]

Or as the great physicist and philosopher Sir Arthur Eddington put it: '. . . the stuff of the world is mind stuff'.[107]

In Vedic Science, consciousness is held to contain the totality of the laws of nature within its scope, rather as an acorn contains, in seed form, the totality of the oak. Vedic Science describes in great detail how consciousness unfolds to create our familiar universe of flowers, clouds, horses, people and trees. When we are aware of the outside world, our consciousness takes on the qualities of the objects we are perceiving rather like a screen takes on the image thrown by a projector. It is possible to experience pure consciousness, in which we simply experience the screen, consciousness itself. This is a deeply fulfilling experience, as Cresswell Jones is even now discovering.

As consciousness unfolds to create the objects we call our world, certain patterns recur. The three doshas are an example of such repeated patterns. People, food, furniture, the weather, everything can be understood in terms of the three doshas. Think of a few of your friends and family. Can you think of anyone who is rather lean and thin, creative, perhaps intellectual? If a male, does he wear a tweed jacket with leather patches where his elbows have worn through? Is he an enthusiast? Maybe a great friend today, then rather distant and aloof another day?

If so, then your friend is displaying (and indeed is somewhat of a caricature) of the Vata personality.

Vata Qualities

Each dosha has its admirable qualities. When Vata is well balanced the subject experiences mental clarity, creative thoughts, enthusiasm and vivacity, sound sleep and good digestion. The qualities of Vata are: *dry, cold, light*.

If Vata is in excess in a particular person's physiology, then that person will feel discomfort. The type of discomfort they feel will reflect an excess of the above qualities. Thus, Vata out of balance manifests as excessive dryness. This could be in the form of dry skin (eczema), dry mouth, dry bowels (constipation), dry joints (osteoarthritis) or even a dry wit!

Similarly when Vata is out of balance the subject feels coldness. Vata dislikes the winter season and may have circulation problems, cold hands and feet. The lightness of Vata when Vata is out of balance could manifest as a loss of body weight, or, since the distinction between mind and body is not as rigid in the Vedic approach as in Western thought, it could be seen as a 'lightweight' type of personality, perhaps not so committed or serious. It could also be seen in a tendency to irregularity—irregularity of daily routine, or for example of hunger, bowel movements or menstruation.

Vata is expressed in cold, dry, windy weather. A person who has a preponderance of Vata will feel the symptoms of Vata more in Vata weather because even more Vata is being added to what is already present in their make-up.

Similarly Vata food will have the qualities of cold, dry and light. Those with much Vata will tend not to like this kind of food. It will make them feel uncomfortable, and they will experience symptoms of Vata excess, because again, too much of the qualities of Vata will be added to the Vata that is already present. According to the principle of opposites, people with a lot of Vata enjoy foods that have the opposite qualities to those of Vata, for example, *hot, moist, heavy*.

A heavy plum pudding will soothe the person with a Vata imbalance and help him or her to feel settled and 'anchored'.

On the other hand, apart from the quality of heat, a heavy plum pudding will not suit at all someone who has a preponderance of Kapha, and even less if that person has a Kapha imbalance.

Kapha Qualities

The qualities associated with Kapha are: *cold, moist, heavy*.

Your Kapha friends will be of bigger build, strong, possessing great stamina and reliability. They may not be so imaginative as those who have Vata present, but they will be dependable.

The sort of food they will feel comfortable eating will have the opposite qualities to those of Kapha. They will tend to like foods that are: *hot, dry, light*.

A Mexican tostada might be a good example.

When Kapha goes out of balance, then the person reflects an excess of the Kapha qualities. He or she may become overweight, sluggish and lazy. The 'couch potato' is the typical out-of-balance Kapha.

Pitta Qualities

Pitta, as we have already mentioned, is the dosha associated with energy. Your Pitta friends will be energetic types, entrepreneurs and leaders. The qualities associated with Pitta are: *hot, dry, light*.

So the sort of food they will like eating will tend to be: *cold, moist, heavy*.

Ice-cream is the classic Pitta pacifying food!

Understanding Your Doshic Make-up

How does one know what doshas one has in one's make-up? The first thing to understand is that *we all have all three*. It is a question of balance among the three doshas.

It is also important to appreciate that the above description of the doshas is highly simplified. It is designed to give the general idea. However, each dosha has five subdoshas, each with their own physiological role, so the permutations and combinations among the doshas and their subdoshas leads to considerable complexity. Furthermore, the doshas can be in balance or out of balance. If out of balance they can be in excess or depleted. When your doshas are in balance, the combination of doshas is referred to as your Prakriti. To put it in simple terms, your Prakriti is your inherent nature, your basic constitution. The extent to which your doshas are out of balance is referred to as Vikriti. Your Vikriti is the degree to which you deviate from your nature.

How to know your Prakriti and Vikriti? There are a number of ways.

First there are the time-honoured methods used by doctors since antiquity: history-taking and examination. History-taking means asking the patient questions about him or herself. Earlier we saw the types of observations Hippocrates liked to make on his patients. The consultant in Maharishi's Vedic Approach to Health can be even more detailed. He or she might ask questions which range widely across your likes, dislikes and life experiences.

How well do you sleep? Is your appetite strong, weak or irregular? Do you prefer summer or winter? Do you sleep soundly or is sleep light and interrupted? Among foods, which tastes do you prefer? Do you rush into things or do you tend to put things off? Do you remember your dreams? In colour? What do you dream about? What kind of exercise do you prefer? The consultant will also be noting your hair colour, skin tones and other physical features such as body build (see Figure 5).

Figure 5: The Three Doshas

Those who have a preponderance of Vata tend to be slimmer in build. Those with more Pitta are medium in build, while Kapha is heavier.

Books are available that list such questions and features in a way that you can try to estimate your Prakriti. I do not recommend this, as it is easy to become confused. Lacking an understanding of the subtleties involved people tend to either get conflicting answers and give up in despair, or they get 'locked' into a perception of themselves as either Vata, Pitta or Kapha. Having decided they are, say, Kapha, they become despondent that they can never eat cucumbers again! It is easy to forget that the doshas are underlying patterns, currents within the ever-changing flux of forms and phenomena. Although these patterns are basic and primordial, we do not want to freeze ourselves too rigidly into one or the other, for then we would be back to being Cnidians again!

> . . . you have privileged access to feelings and perceptions about yourself that no one else can experience in exactly the same way.

This does not mean that one's own perceptions and experience are not useful in diagnosis. In fact you have privileged access to feelings and perceptions about yourself that no one else can experience in exactly the same way. There is no harm in noticing, for example, that sleep is lighter than normal. This is a valuable clue to a Vata imbalance. As one gains familiarity with the Vedic system of health, the degree of *weight* to be put on such perceptions will become more obvious, so that you will be able to use them to paint a broad and comprehensive picture of yourself. This is our Coan aim, rather than limit ourselves to one or two categories.

Diagnosis by the Pulse

The consultant trained in the Vedic system can also gain a great deal of information by a very refined method of examination called pulse diagnosis. Taking the pulse has been an emblem of the doctor's art since antiquity. As Western doctors we note the rate and rhythm of the pulse. We also recognise that there are differences in the character of the pulse from one patient to another. Thus a 'slow rising pulse' may indicate the condition of aortic stenosis in which the flow from the heart is impeded by a faulty aortic valve. Most of the conditions recognisable by the pulse in Western medicine nowadays are conditions of gross illness and the art of diagnosis by the pulse is relatively crude.

This has not always been the case. As recently as 1875, a Professor Broadbent of St Mary's Hospital was able to discourse to his students on the 'small, long and hard' pulse which he associated with kidney disease and gout, and the 'short, quick, shabby' pulse he saw in conditions such as 'melancholia', epilepsy and acute dementia.[108]

The great Greek physician Galen, who lived in the first century AD, is said to have described 27 different forms of the pulse. Pulse diagnosis is practised in Chinese medicine as well as in the Indian tradition of Ayurveda. Clearly it has a long and hallowed history and has been respected throughout the ages in many different cultures. What caused us in the West to lose interest in this valuable means of gaining information?

Perhaps the following quotation from *The Lancet* of 1911 will give us a clue:

> ... the modern spirit, inspired by science, with its universal passion for measurement, has touched the pulse as it has touched many other

commonplace objects and movements . . . the ambition, in short, of instrumental methods . . . is to describe the pulse in terms of measurement . . . [109]

By measuring the pressure of the pulse with our sphygmomanometer and losing interest in its character, we gained precision but lost our appreciation of its richness. The word 'measure' in its modern sense usually implies comparison of an object with an external standard or unit. Thus if you want to measure your waist, you wrap a tape measure around your tummy and read off so many standard bits, centimetres or inches, which our reductivist forebears, by breaking length up into units, have conveniently defined for us.

There is another, deeper sense of measure, of which our current use of the word is probably a trivialisation. This deeply Coan meaning survives only when we use expressions such as 'a measured tread', or doing something 'in good measure'. Here measure means harmony or proper proportion. To the ancient Greeks, to keep everything in its proper measure was essential to health. When something went beyond its proper measure, this meant that it was inwardly out of balance.

Pulse diagnosis has traditionally been a method to 'get the measure' of a patient, by which I mean assess to what degree the patient is inwardly balanced and therefore healthy. We have diluted our rich

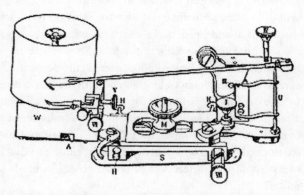

Figure 6: Analysis of the Pulse—the Sphygmograph

The sphygmograph and our familiar sphygmomanometer were developed side by side. Only the sphygmomanometer survived to become standard doctor's office equipment. Even though the sphygmograph has the potential to provide unique information, it gave way to the more easily interpreted electrocardiograph (ECG).

knowledge of the pulse to a mere comparison with the weight of a column of mercury!

This loss did not happen all at once. For many years, the sphygmomanometer existed side by side with another device, the sphygmograph (see Figure 6). The sphygmograph gave a kind of graphic printout of the wave-form of the pulse. The pulse could then be seen to be fast- or slow-rising, peaked or sustained and so forth.

The sphygmograph told us about the character of the pulse. This is much closer to the spirit in which the tradition of pulse diagnosis had thrived. However, the tracings of the pulse wave-forms were difficult to analyse. They could not be broken into little bits or units of measurement very easily and this did not suit the reductivist spirit of the age. By and by the sphygmograph was forgotten (it was replaced by the more easily-measured electrocardiograph or ECG). The sphygmomanometer assumed a dominant role in the doctor's office.

Vedic pulse diagnosis is not a foreign importation into Western medicine, it is a return to roots that lie hidden in our past. How does the Vedic practitioner assess the pulse? While it may be learned at first intellectually, its advanced practice is a process of recognition, a kind of resonance between practitioner and patient in a rather similar way that a mother is at one with her child.

For a loving mother, the import of the cry of her child is somehow innately known. No one had to teach her the characteristics that differentiate the cry associated with boredom from the cry of real distress; those characteristics are immediately obvious to her. For those who are not mothers, or who have not seen a mother in action recently, consider the sound of a car coming down the road. If it were an original Volkswagen 'beetle', most people would be able to instantly recognise its inimitable thrashings and identify it, differentiating it from, say, a later Volkswagen or a car of a different make. This is a form of recognition that is not learned by painstakingly noting and enumerating the qualities of the Volkswagen sound, one by one. It is learned we might say 'by experience', and by noting the 'sound as a whole'.

Skilled practitioners of pulse diagnosis are impressive. I have met traditional Vedic consultants who, after a few seconds of resting their fingers on one's pulse, can give a startlingly accurate summary of how one is feeling, what physical discomforts one is experiencing if any, and what medical difficulties one has had in the past. He or she does this by recognising the quality of the 'pulse as a whole'. Inherent in the simple rise and fall of the pulse is a veritable mine of information that can tell the skilled doctor anything he or she needs to know. The degree of sensitivity that is displayed can be remarkable. It is said that in ancient times, since it was not proper for a male doctor to touch even the pulse of a female patient, the doctor took the pulse from a fine piece of silk wrapped around the lady's wrist and passed out from behind a screen!

This may seem an incredible idea to Western-trained people. It should not seem too surprising when we remember that from our own chaos theory, scientists have discovered a vast amount of hidden information in what appeared to be random fluctuations in the heart rate. Chaologists talk about the pulse rate being 'information rich'. Although the Vedic practitioner analyses the pulse not so much according to its rate, but by its character, the concept of hidden information of a higher order contained within the pulse is the same.

True Preventive Medicine

One of the great advantages of becoming more closely Coan, is in the early recognition of disorder. You may recall that this was the third strategy in our great escape from the drug mentality: find the people who are going to have strokes or heart attacks and treat them preferentially. To the Coan, health is a state of harmony with the rest of the universe. Deviation from this should be evident long before a Cnidian could identify symptoms that would clearly indicate the presence of a disease. History-taking, examination and pulse diagnosis all help to identify early disorder that, while not recognised as disease, nevertheless represents an early state of imbalance that could later manifest itself as disease.

Preventive medicine has been something of a lame duck in medical thought since it does not fit easily into the Cnidian framework. With its emphasis on defining and treating specific diseases and vagueness about what it means to treat the 'whole person', doctors have tended

> Preventive medicine has been something of a lame duck in medical thought . . .

to think of prevention as early treatment of specific diseases, one by one. A piecemeal approach to wholeness is never likely to succeed, and this kind of approach in prevention has led to fragmented and unsatisfactory preventive health strategies. Thus we are enjoined not to drink milk for the sake of our hearts, but to drink milk for the sake of our bones. Wine is good for the heart, says one study, so we should drink it. The depressant effect of alcohol on the central nervous system is disregarded. Mammograms are good for women over 50 (we think), so they should have them regardless of the harmful effect of ionising radiation, while every child should be immunised even though a known proportion of those will suffer neurological damage as a result.

What passes for preventive medicine is really not prevention at all. Cervical screening and mammography, often cited as evidence of our good work in this area, can only be called early detection of disease. By the time the disease is detectable by these methods it may, in many cases, already be well advanced. Sometimes these activities are called 'secondary prevention', but this does not make the situation any better. If someone has a disease by the time you have found it, then you have not prevented it. The term 'secondary prevention' is no more than a smokescreen for our inadequacy in really preventing disease.

The unfortunate state of what passes for preventive health is a consequence not of lack of good will and good intentions, but of lack of knowledge about wholeness. Disease is the absence of health or wholeness. The converse is not true. Health, or wholeness, is not the absence of disease. Therefore it is not possible to create perfect health by chipping away at diseases one by one.

Traditionally, at least six stages in pathogenesis (disease formation) are described in the Vedic system. Only in the last two stages do signs and symptoms recognisable as disease appear, so stages one to four are detected as early imbalances in the patient's doshas. As the Ayurvedic scholar H.S. Kasture states:

> . . . every disease passes through six stages, but we only know it when the signs and symptoms are well manifested in the fifth state . . . A wise . . . physician can understand the subtle changes in the body and come to know the proper stage and he will be very successful in controlling a patient's problems in a timely manner, without complications. [110]

Thus a Vata imbalance may at first simply manifest as a tendency to worry or to feel the cold. More advanced Vata imbalance could give rise to conditions such as insomnia or anxiety. Finally, a severe Vata imbalance could manifest as a neurological condition such as Parkinson's disease or multiple sclerosis. A Pitta imbalance may begin as a tendency to anger, then manifest as dyspepsia. The relatively undifferentiated symptom of dyspepsia may later develop into peptic ulceration. Kapha disorders take a long time to develop, but once established are slow to improve. A Kapha imbalance may first manifest simply as a tendency to laziness or indolence. Later manifestations of Kapha disorder include certain types of obesity, non-insulin-dependent diabetes and tumours.

Which doshas are out of balance in hypertension? We can gain a clue from an interesting finding reported in the same *Lancet* of 1911 which describes the sphygmomanometer and sphygmograph. Doctors at that time found that the pressure as measured by the sphygmomanometer did not correspond very well with the different types of wave-form as measured by the sphygmograph. Sometimes a patient with high blood pressure might have a tall, spiky trace, while another with the same pressure reading might have a smaller, more stubby trace (see Figure 7). This puzzled them. Since pulse diagnosis is all about the shape of the wave form, it might suggest to us, however, that hypertension can be present in many different combinations of the doshas, and in fact this seems to be correct. Although typically hypertension is a Vata or a Pitta problem, it can also occur in Kapha disorders.

This is a phenomenon often seen in the practice of Maharishi's Vedic Approach to Health. Two people might present to a practitioner with the same (Cnidian-defined) disease, asthma, for example. In the West, they are very likely to be treated with the same drugs. This is because in the West, we treat the disease. The Vedic consultant might treat the two people with asthma very differently, depending on the balance or imbalance of the doshas present. He treats the person. If Kapha is imbalanced the person might be advised to take more exercise, for example. If Vata is the problem, then heavy exercise might make the asthma worse.

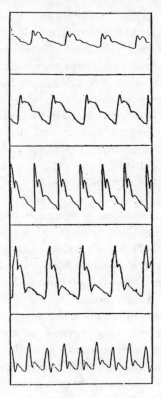

Figure 7: Same Pressure, Different People

This figure shows the sphygmograms of five individuals. Notice how different they are, yet they all have the same blood pressure. While blood pressure gives us some information about an individual, the wave form of the pulse contains richer information. (Sphygmogram reproduced courtesy of *The Lancet*).[109]

Similarly, in the West we treat hypertension, but for the Vedic consultant the correct procedure is to treat the doshic imbalance. From the Vedic point of view, once the doshas are in balance, the blood pressure takes care of itself. Of course this can be checked by regular monitoring.

It follows also that, since any of three doshas can be involved, the 'personality' of the typical hypertensive can vary. Those with a Vata imbalance will tend to be anxious and of a worrying nature. Cresswell

Jones fits this type. Because Vata is the principle of movement, their blood pressure might tend to be erratic, high when measured on some days and normal on others. This kind of hypertension is called 'labile hypertension'. Those with a Pitta imbalance might fit the classic image of the plethoric and irascible army colonel, of whom many of us think when we picture the hypertensive. (Pitta is all to do with discipline and order, so is often well represented in the armed forces!) If Kapha is preponderant, then high blood pressure might be expected to be sustained, slower to respond to treatment and perhaps associated with lethargy and fluid retention.

Meanwhile, back to Cresswell Jones . . .

Aaron, his Transcendental Meditation teacher, had told Cresswell that learning Transcendental Meditation is not like learning to play the piano or the violin—it does not take years before you are any good. Most people notice results very early, usually within the first two weeks—enough to convince them that this is something genuine and worth continuing. The benefits are cumulative from then on. 'We are all different,' says Aaron, 'and some people take a few more days than others to notice the benefits.' Cresswell had promptly put himself firmly in the camp of 'non-achievers'. In fact one of his main concerns was that he would be the first person for whom the technique simply wouldn't work! He is therefore quite unprepared for the immediacy of the relaxation when he first tries the technique. His first impulse is to laugh with delight. He remembers just in time that he is a 47-year-old accountant, married and wearing a grey suit.

One month later, and Cresswell is convinced that Transcendental Meditation must be helping keep his blood pressure down. He feels so much better! But how will he know it has improved? Before he started Transcendental Meditation the blood pressure was OK, but that was because of the pills. Now that he is doing Transcendental Meditation the blood pressure is still OK. Are his pills necessary any longer? Cresswell decides the only thing to do is to take the bull by the horns. Front up to Feldstein and demand that he withdraws these pills. He is not looking forward to this, because Dr Feldstein told him to stay on them for the rest of his life, and Dr Feldstein is, well, a very learned and rather forceful man. Nevertheless, as he tells Ellen, a stand has to be made. He will be firm and direct. Even pound the desk if necessary. He is prepared to take the risk. Feldstein will just have to accept that it's his body, after all.

Unbeknown to Cresswell, Dr Feldstein has also been doing some reading. A circular entitled 'Healthy Scepticism' came through the mail.[111] It contained a lot of material about the methods used to convince doctors to prescribe drugs. Maybe he does need to be more on the alert. A lot of the country's money is at stake after all. One has to be responsible. He hears talk too about 'Step Down Therapy', matching the dose of a drug to the patient's response so that they can get by on the smallest dose possible. Maybe he does need to look at this a little. He checks his appointment book. Next patient is Jones. Now there's a man who's never very happy taking medication. He might just be a good candidate for step-down therapy. Titrate the dose to the response, that's the thing. Thus it is that when Cresswell diffidently brings up the matter of perhaps reducing the dose of his tablets just a little, to his extreme surprise Feldstein concurs immediately! Together they decide to halve the dose and meet again in a week.

A week goes by. Feldstein measures carefully. Jones' blood pressure is 140/82, more or less the same as the previous week on twice the dose. The good doctor suggests they should be happy with that, but Cresswell has the scent of victory in his nostrils and insists on stopping altogether. A week later the reading is 145/85, and the week after that 142/80. Cresswell is jubilant, Feldstein cautious. The following week it is 165/90. Cresswell is crestfallen and expects Feldstein to reinstate medication. However, Feldstein suggests another reading in a week's time and advises Cresswell to continue with his 'non-pharmacological interventions'.

Jones is not so sure about those interventions now. He didn't enjoy them half so much as he is enjoying Transcendental Meditation. Losing weight, physical exercise, stopping smoking, getting cholesterol down and avoiding salt? How do they fit in with Maharishi's Vedic Approach to Health? He is eager to find out.

As we have seen, speaking statistically, there is very little doubt that average blood pressure within a population can be lowered if the population loses weight, gets some exercise and lowers the average salt intake. The problem for Cresswell is that he did not seem to particularly enjoy his jogging and salt-free diet. Without understanding his doshic make-up, this could be very frustrating to his doctor, who might see it as his duty to convince Cresswell that jogging and a meagre ration of salt were for 'his own good'.

The epidemiologist's dilemma is just as acute in considering the evidence for non-pharmacological measures as in the other areas we have already considered. We know it would be better if everyone ate less salt, but, since it might not help each individual, can we insist on this? Thinking as Coans, can our knowledge of the doshas help here?

According to Maharishi's Vedic Approach to Health, there are six main tastes in our food. Three of the six possible tastes 'pacify' Vata. In this context 'pacify' means to relieve a Vata excess. These tastes are sweet, sour and salty. The other three tastes (pungent, bitter and astringent) pacify Kapha. Pitta is pacified by sweet, bitter and astringent tastes.

We already have enough evidence to suspect that Jones is strong in the Vata dosha, with a distinct Vata excess. He worries, he dashes around, he forgets things, he doesn't sleep well. All these traits signify excessive Vata.

I once met a patient who admitted to scooping up salt from a bag and eating it directly from his hands. This sort of salt intake is not good for any of us. Nevertheless salt, when not taken to that sort of excess, is beneficial in calming or 'pacifying' Vata, according to Vedic wisdom. Cresswell will feel drawn to salty foods and find them satisfying. In attempting a salt-free diet, he will feel pinched and unsatisfied. What about his blood pressure? Remember, in the Japanese study we discussed earlier, fully 60 percent of the population were unaffected by an enormously high intake of salt. According to the Vedic knowledge, those with hypertension caused by Pitta or Kapha imbalance are the most likely to develop blood pressure problems by taking salt in excess. Conversely, a low-salt diet will feel comfortable and satisfying to them.

Am I not taking a risk, recommending that some people take more salt than others, when the studies show such a close association between a population's average salt intake and its average blood pressure? Not really. Remember that some people's blood pressure actually rises with salt depletion. It is really the epidemiologists who are taking the risk! Apart from that, blood pressure is easily monitored. On reading this, you might decide that you have a Vata imbalance and need more salt. If, on taking more salt, your blood pressure rises, then you need to stop taking salt and question your doshic diagnosis!

Vata, being the dosha associated with movement, is not well suited to the bodily movement associated with very heavy exercise (a dosha is pushed out of balance when more of its own qualities are imposed from outside). Again a moderate amount of exercise is good for us all, but heavy exercise will tend to create strain in one of a Vata preponderance. Jones disliked jogging, but a hypertensive with a Kapha imbalance would probably thrive on it. Jones should do some exercise, maybe forty minutes of brisk walking three times a week, but he should not exercise to the point of strain—nobody should.

There are many complexities to the three-dosha theory that cannot be covered in this book; however, speaking simplistically, excess weight, or obesity, is a Kapha imbalance. It is recognised in Vedic knowledge that those with a Kapha preponderance will naturally be of bigger, more solid build and will carry weight with grace and ease. It is not necessary for us all to have legs as thin as sparrows' for the sake of our hearts! However, there is a point at which excess weight is not good for anybody, and this is why statistical studies show quite un-equivocally that one of the best things to bring high blood pressure down is to reduce weight, when the subject is carrying more weight than is comfortable.[112]

While this is recognised in the West, it is notoriously difficult for many obese people to lose weight in a sustained way. Here again, the Vedic approach can be very helpful.

Kim was a 40-year-old glazier who learned Transcendental Meditation to help him cope with the stress of running a small business. He was quite markedly overweight, a problem he had had for years and had not been able to overcome. Although he had tried many diets, the harder he tried, the harder it seemed to be to lose weight permanently. Three weeks after learning Transcendental Meditation he rang me to tell me delightedly that he had lost four kilograms! This had happened spontaneously. Somehow, for Kim, the awareness had grown that in the end it is not much fun to be overweight, even though in the short term it is fun to eat food. The mind is spontaneously drawn towards enjoyment. Once it is clear to the mind that greater fun is to be had by being normal weight than is to be had in the short term by eating more, the choice to eat less becomes easy. Kim did not think this out consciously, the process occurred spontaneously at the preconscious level of refined mental activity. To Kim it simply came as a delightful surprise.

What About Cholesterol?

The cholesterol story! So far, in this book I have not talked much about the companion demon that, along with hypertension, got planted in the public mind. I approach it now with trepidation, knowing that it could very easily be the single subject of another, longer book! Suffice to say that if the epidemiologist's dilemma has led to debate in the treatment of hypertension, then that is a minor skirmish compared to the cholesterol imbroglio, with its dogmatic pronouncements and abrupt reversals. Should we eat eggs or not? Five years ago, definitely not. Now it seems we can.[113] If the general public is left reeling and confused, this is not surprising since 'significant confusion exists among health care professionals' as well.[114]

Within this scene of disarray I would like to emphasise the following points:

1. Cholesterol is a necessary substance for the body.
2. Most blood cholesterol is produced by the liver. Only about one-third comes from our diet.
3. Cholesterol in the blood can be lowered by a low-fat diet, but most studies show that dietary cholesterol itself plays only a minor role in raising blood cholesterol. Thus it is that, at least from the scientific point of view, egg yolks, which are high in cholesterol, are again 'OK'.
4. The evidence against high blood cholesterol is statistical. Just as we saw in hypertension, we know with near certainty that if a population has an elevated average blood cholesterol, then that population will have a high incidence of heart disease. But we

don't know enough about people to be able to say which individuals will have the heart problems. Plenty of people with high cholesterol have lived to a ripe old age. The majority of heart attacks occur among people whose blood cholesterol is normal.

5. A high blood cholesterol is a statistical risk factor for heart disease and stroke, and should therefore be taken into account along with all other risk factors, such as high blood pressure and smoking. The pressure to treat high blood cholesterol with drugs is becoming increasingly strong at increasingly lower levels of cholesterol, just as occurred in hypertension. It may not be necessary or even beneficial for everyone to lower their· cholesterol. A review of a large number of trials found that men whose cholesterol levels were below 4.14 mmol/l exhibited 20 percent more cancer deaths, 35 percent more deaths from injury, 40 percent more non-cardiovascular, non-cancer deaths, and 50 percent more deaths from digestive system disease.[115]

6. The way in which cholesterol is transported in the individual's blood is important. Low-density lipoprotein (LDL) seems to be the 'baddie' among the transport proteins. This is particularly true when it is in its oxidised form. (Rancid butter is oxidised butter, so we could perhaps think of oxidised LDL as 'rancid' LDL.) Antioxida-nts are substances that convert oxidised molecules back into non-oxidised molecules. Fresh vegetables and fruits contain anti-oxidants. Several studies have shown that a whole-food diet rich in anti-oxidants gives some protection from atherosclerosis. However, direct supplementation of the diet with an artificial single-molecule anti-oxidant such as beta carotene did not. Nature already knew best, just as we saw in the DASH study in which whole foods were found to be beneficial in hypertension. Whole foods contain something that is 'more than the sum of the parts' that we do not find in artificial substitutes. That 'something more' makes all the difference. If it is true (and it seems increasingly likely that it is) that oxidised low-density lipoprotein cholesterol is a major culprit in the formation of atherosclerosis, then a Maharishi

Vedic food supplement known as Amrit Kalash may provide a better solution to the cholesterol problem than blanket cholesterol lowering. This preparation has been the subject of intensive study by Professor Hari Sharma, emeritus professor at Ohio State University College of Medicine, and his group of co-workers.[116] Made according to an ancient recipe using plants carefully harvested and prepared, it has been shown to be a very powerful anti-oxidant indeed. Dr Sharma's work has sparked further studies on this compound in laboratories in India, Russia, Japan and Holland.

7. The regular practise of Transcendental Meditation has been associated with lower levels of lipid peroxides (oxidised lipids) in one exploratory study.[117]

Treating the Coan Way

Lying on the Abhyanga table Cresswell Jones imagines he might be in heaven. Specially prepared Vata pacifying oil scents the air as he stretches out luxuriously. He has been receiving a full body massage as part of Maharishi Panchakarma. Abhyanga literally means 'a helping hand' and today four helping hands belonging to two well-trained male technicians have been efficiently massaging his middle-aged body, one on either side of him, their strokes sure and perfectly co-ordinated. Now he is having Shirodhara, in which oil is poured from a container above continuously on to his forehead and allowed to stream across his scalp and face. Panchakarma was in ancient times known as 'the Royal Treatment'. He could believe that!

So far we have talked mainly about Coan diagnosis. What about Coan treatment?

If the doshas are found to be out of balance, then treatment involves correction of the doshic imbalance. In this way the patient receives exactly the right treatment for him or her. We have seen already that one of the main methods to correct imbalances among the doshas is through our diet. In Maharishi's Vedic Approach to Health, food is analysed not so much according to its molecular structure, but according to the manner in which its taste and quality influence the doshas. We have already seen that the salty taste reduces Vata, for example. Herbal food supplements are used in a similar way. Adjustments to our lifestyle, the best time to get up, the best times to eat and so forth, are also useful in 'pacifying' the doshas. The very effective and specialised kind of purification treatment that Cresswell has just had, known as Maharishi Panchakarma, may also be available in your area.

A course of Panchakarma is a uniquely rejuvenating experience. Maharishi Panchakarma is a highly systematised series of steps involving oil, massage, heat and elimination procedures designed to rid the body of impurities. In the Vedic system, these impurities are understood in terms of excess of one or more doshas.

Simple changes to your diet are among the easiest ways to 'pacify' a dosha or doshas. As mentioned, here the 'principle of opposites' applies. A dosha in excess is pacified by the opposite qualities to its own. The qualities of Vata, for example, are cold, light and dry. So Vata is pacified by warm, heavier, moist food. A lasagne, for example, would pacify a Vata excess. A Pitta imbalance is best treated with cool, moist foods such as melons or cucumber. Those of Kapha preponderance need to be careful about not eating to excess and should favour a lighter diet. Your local Maharishi Vedic consultant can help you decide on a suitable diet for you.

Herbal Templates

Vedic science includes a compendious knowledge of herbal species and how they can help restore the body to a state of health. Some of these herbs, such as rauwolfia, have been taken into the Western pharmacopoeia, their 'active ingredients' isolated and made into Western drugs. Thus the drug reserpine, isolated from the rauwolfia plant, was one of the first drugs used in the West for hypertension and continues to be used today, particularly in the United States.[118]

Herbal food supplements, when taken to correct doshic imbalances, can be very effective. Although their function, like all Maharishi Vedic interventions, is to gently nudge the body back into balance, they should not be thought so gentle as to be ineffective. As mentioned in our chapter on pharmacology, I have frequently had success from

herbal preparations when Western pharmaceuticals have failed. Nigel
is another example, a middle-aged librarian who came to my practice
after having been told by his doctor that he would need to take blood
pressure tablets for the rest of his life. Being primarily of a studious
nature, Nigel felt disinclined towards exercise and took as little of it as
possible. He was somewhat overweight. He had tried cutting down on
salt, and he had tried acupuncture, both to no effect. His pulse
indicated a Vata imbalance consistent with mental overexertion.

I had planned to get a series of blood pressure readings over a
month to get an idea of Nigel's baseline readings, but on his third visit,
his blood pressure had risen from the initial readings of 130/100 to
180/130. Nigel was complaining of vague, dizzy feelings 'as if he had
had a couple of drinks'. Things, I felt, had gone far enough. Nigel had
what is known as accelerated hypertension, a slippery path to
malignant hypertension. I decided to start him on an ACE inhibitor. I
also arranged for him to see a specialist physician in case he had one
of the rarer causes of secondary hypertension. One month later, on a
full dose of ACE inhibitor as well as a diuretic added by the specialist,
Nigel still was not doing very well. Blood pressure continued to hover
around the 155/100 mark. I decided to add a herbal supplement from
Maharishi's Vedic Approach to Health. Beginning with a small dose,
his blood pressure responded and within a week was 126/92. I then
began increasing the herb and decreasing the ACE inhibitor. This all
happened about seven years ago. Nigel is by no means a star patient.
In spite of my encouragement he has not managed to lose any weight
nor does he get any exercise to speak of. However, his blood pressure,
measured recently at 120/86, is quite satisfactory. At the time of writing
he takes no ACE inhibitor and no diuretic and his blood pressure
improvement appears to be solely owing to the herbal preparation he
takes each day, since it rises if he stops taking it.

Are the Vedic herbs not then primitive 'drugs'? This is certainly the
view taken by most Western pharmacologists. However, it is to miss
the point for which these herbs are given.

One of the consequences of the great move towards reductivism in
the seventeenth century was to try to reduce medicines to their 'active
ingredients' and discard anything that was considered to be

superfluous. Western pharmacology thus tries to keep things simple by adhering to a 'one disease, one therapeutic molecule' principle. Vedic herbal food supplements are not intended to have one specific chemical effect, but in fact have multiple chemical effects on the body as a whole. The very complexity of the interactions with the body of the various component chemicals in the herb is important. The synergy among these components is said to act as a kind of template, or example to the body, of how it is to order itself. Vedic Science teaches that the chemical constituents of a herb act together to create a 'whole that is greater than the parts'.

As Professor Hari Sharma puts it:

> Those of us who do medical research aren't used to taking whole flowers, plants and roots and grinding them down into an unanalyzed *potpourri* of various substances. Rather, we are used to seeking for a single active ingredient, a magic bullet to fire at each disease . . . The ancient herbal food supplements from [Maharishi's Vedic Approach to Health are] . . . a rich stew of molecules intended to enrich the human physiology in its entirety. There is no attempt to isolate individual molecules and these supplements are in no sense drugs . . . recent scientific experiments have shown these formulas to be dramatically effective—with virtually no side-effects.[119]

The simplicity of the Vedic system of pharmacology comes not from considering the molecular components of a herbal species, but by considering the effect the plant has on the doshas. The doshas are held to be more fundamental to life than molecules. By attending to the doshas we can cut through the complexity of the chemical reactions. For the majority of Maharishi Vedic herbal food supplements, the effects on the doshas can quite simply be predicted by the taste and quality of the preparation, just as in the case of foods. There is no need for an expensive laboratory, no rows of test-tubes, no white-coated technicians. You already have a superb 'doshic laboratory'—your tongue.

Since the preparations are designed to enrich the 'physiology in its entirety', the incidence of side-effects from Maharishi Vedic herbal food supplements is low. One study carried out by Professor Sharma on a Maharishi Vedic preparation showed only minor side-effects— mild rash and gastro-intestinal disturbance among 5 percent of subjects which responded to reduced dosage. Standard blood tests showed no toxic effects.[119]

Of course some plants are poisonous. Just because a preparation is plant-based does not guarantee its safety. However, the formulae of Maharishi's Vedic Approach to Health are based on the experience of many thousands of years. Similarly, some herbs can be very powerful. This is recognised in Vedic Science. A special group of herbs are said to have effects that override those derived from their taste and quality. These singular, and often powerful, effects are known as *prabhava* effects. Rauwolfia is an example of a substance that exerts a prabhava effect, another is digitalis. Both have been appropriated by Western medicine since, in the West, short-term results are sought after, and the long-term value of the more gentle, nourishing herbal food supplements have not been appreciated. Rauwolfia can be a very useful herb in the treatment of hypertension, but it should be used with care and in expert combination with other herbs, since it can have undesirable effects in some people. Its so-called 'active ingredient' reserpine, still used in the West, has also been noted to give similar side-effects in some cases, notably depression and nasal stuffiness. For this reason, rauwolfia and reserpine are usually restricted drugs that can be prescribed only by a medical practitioner in most countries.

On a note of caution also, some suppliers who advertise 'ayurvedic preparations' may lack the background knowledge needed to prepare these compounds properly or in proper combinations, nor may the plants involved have been harvested in the meticulous way prescribed by the ancient recipes, so that the preparations are not very effective. Herbal preparations from Maharishi's Vedic Approach to Health are carefully prepared and have been field-tested for thousands of years, far longer and by many more people than could be possible in the short span of time that is available to test a Western drug.

Sometimes herbal preparations in general are criticised in that a drug can be more easily standardised than a multi-molecular herb. However, herbal preparations can now be 'fingerprinted' using modern scientific methods such as liquid chromatography. This allows you to be confident that what you see on the label is what is actually in the bottle.

Active ingredients of other naturally occurring substances have been used in the West to treat hypertension (the ACE inhibitors use a substance first extracted from the venom of a snake, the South American pit viper). ACE inhibitors bring blood pressure down (in about 60 percent of individuals), but do not necessarily help the person beyond the advantages of a lower blood pressure. Preparations from Maharishi's Vedic Approach to Health are designed to heal the person deeply so that normal blood pressure is the natural result. A consequence of this is that very often such preparations can, after a time, be withdrawn or reduced to a very small dose, without return to the hypertensive state. Whereas Western drugs aim to lower blood pressure, Vedic herbs aim to heal.

The Bottom Line is Feeling Good

Whatever balances the doshas feels good to the subject. Imbalanced doshas feel uncomfortable and the person does not feel happy. In a confused world we tend to be guided in our behaviour by all kinds of arbitrary advice on what we should eat and how we should conduct our daily routine. This comes first from parents, grandparents and schoolteachers, then later from doctors, public health authorities and peers. We often hear, for example, that we should all eat a good breakfast. When I ask a group of say twenty people, 'Who thinks we should all have a good breakfast in the morning?' all hands go up. But when I ask, 'How many people here actually enjoy eating breakfast?' usually about two-thirds of the hands go down! In the Vedic system, contrary to all that our grandmothers may have told us, breakfast is the least important meal of the day and should only be eaten if enjoyed. Go by how you feel.

> . . . we need only ask ourselves the simple, bottom-line question: 'Am I feeling good?'

Trust the Body

Writing in *The Heart Single Field Theory*, Jaques Boivin says:

> If we wish to understand the nature of the Universe we have an inner hidden advantage: we are ourselves little portions of the universe and so carry the answer within us.[120]

One of the most significant features of Vedic Science is that we get the best information from within ourselves. We can trust our own physiology to tell us what is best for us. No one has to tell a cat to eat grass when it is sick; it seems to know this instinctively. Ask yourself, 'Do I enjoy eating breakfast? Do I feel better for it?' Your own body is your best guide. In the West we are often out of touch with our instincts and our intuitions. We can use our self-knowledge to guide us into new patterns of behaviour. In general, for all new interventions, we need only ask ourselves the simple, bottom-line question: 'Am I feeling good? Do I feel light and happy as a result?' If the answer is yes, then the new behaviour, whether it be a form of exercise, a changed diet or going to bed earlier, is likely to be the right behaviour for you.

Replace One Habit with a Better One

Naturally we have to take into account the force of habits entrenched in our behaviour. However, as we saw in the case of Kim, who spontaneously began to eat more appropriately, bad habits tend to drop away as awareness grows. As we become familiar with finer states of thought and the broadened awareness associated with pure consciousness, the ability to make choices increases.

'Normally I would have smoked forty, but today I only smoked fifteen!'

This process, called refinement of desire, I have observed to be beneficial in many types of addictions, be they to food, alcohol, cigarettes or work. Alex was an architect in his mid-fifties, who learned Transcendental Meditation some years ago. He approached me on the second day of instruction, saying, with a beaming smile, 'In a few months, I think this Transcendental Meditation will have paid for itself.' 'How so?' I asked. 'Well,' he said, 'this afternoon my cigarette case and cigarette lighter were sitting on my desk, same as usual. Normally I would have smoked forty, but today I only smoked fifteen!'

This is a not uncommon story. People who have smoked heavily for years will find themselves going down to the corner store less often to pick up their cigarettes, after they have learned Transcendental Meditation. A half-empty packet remains in their jacket unused. Often people will give up smoking altogether in this way, or they will find it much easier to follow the advice given in a standard 'stopping smoking' course. Formal studies among meditators confirm that the habit becomes less compelling as the subject continues to meditate regularly.[121]

Towards Perfect Health

The *Sushruta Samhita*, an ancient Vedic text, gives this definition of a healthy, or whole, person:

> He whose doshas are in balance, whose appetite is good, whose dhatus [bodily tissues] are functioning normally, whose malas [products of excretion] are in balance, and whose Self, mind and senses remain full of bliss, is called a healthy person. (Sush. Su. 15.38)[122]

In helping my patients master the skill of transcending thought, I find that with the sense of wholeness that the patient develops, comes a deeper sense of self. With this comes a sense of inner contentment, bliss, the joy of coming back to oneself.

We can learn to trust our desires as awareness grows and unhelpful habits drop away. Then our knowledge of the doshas can help satisfy the intellect that our behaviour is indeed upon the right lines as we grow towards perfect health.

The Plan in Place

Thus we have in place two of our three escape strategies to free ourselves from the epidemiologist's dilemma and the tyranny of drugs. The first is the universal technique for creating wholeness, Transcendental Meditation. So far in this chapter we have outlined our second strategy. The second strategy was to find therapies that 'fit the person', rather than making the same recommendation for all. The three-dosha system of Maharishi's Vedic Approach to Health allows us to appreciate and respect the diversity that exists among us and treat each person uniquely.

How far can we push this Coan idea? Our third strategy was to identify in advance those likely to have strokes or heart attacks and treat them long before the problem arose. Using our knowledge of the three doshas, could we really predict in advance exactly which people are in line for a heart attack, perhaps even without recourse to measuring blood pressure, blood cholesterol or any other Western measure?

While, to my knowledge, there have been no formal studies done, it seems very likely that a skilled *Vaidya* (one traditionally trained in diagnosis according to Maharishi's Vedic Approach to Health) could recognise early signs that might lead to heart disease long before any of the above signs were present. He or she might not necessarily name this 'early heart disease', though. This is partly because there is less of a tendency to 'name' in the Vedic system, but mainly because the imbalance is likely to be undifferentiated at that stage, manifesting not as a problem specifically related to the heart, but as an excess or depletion of one or other doshas or subdoshas. The Vaidya could then give recommendations that would help to create proper doshic balance and help to avert the danger even before the heart was targeted.

I am well aware that in expounding the virtues of pulse diagnosis and the three-dosha system from Maharishi's Vedic Approach to Health, I stray from the comfortable kind of evidence-based territory which many of my colleagues prefer. I hope that my exposition of the limitations of epidemiological research has made clear my reasons for doing so. Orthodox medicine has become so enamoured of population evidence that it has almost completely forgotten that we are treating people. We need to become more person-oriented, to understand people deeply. It behoves us to expand our philosophy and become more Coan. As doctors and as patients we need to study with sincerity the teachings that come to us from other cultures, rather than attempt to force them through our own conceptual sieve. We will find a rich vein of knowledge that complements our own perfectly. This takes humility, but we will be rewarded to find that the Vedic knowledge speaks to us just as powerfully as it has to countless cultures in ages past. The knowledge of the Veda is universal. Einstein's Theory of Relativity was formulated by a German Jew, but we do not think of it as German, Jewish knowledge. It is universal knowledge that applies to all. Vedic knowledge belongs not only to India, but to all cultures.

Does this mean we should stop being Cnidians, then? Earlier, we noted that Hippocrates, while a superb Coan, also combined the Cnidian approach in a masterly way. The two are not opposing views, but complementary, and we would not like to throw out the baby with the Cnidian bathwater. The Cnidian stream of thought is a valuable tool, as long as it is appropriately applied. Indeed, elements of the Cnidian method are present in the Veda, in a section known as Nyaya. A chisel does not make a good hammer, nor should it be used as a screwdriver. By being predominantly Cnidian in medicine, we have tended to use one tool for all purposes. That is not good, but we can still use the tool for the purpose for which it was designed.

Provided we keep in mind that our Cnidian categories are simply conventions and don't allow them to appropriate a life of their own, the Cnidian approach gives us ease of communication and precision of thought. Sometimes naming a disease can be reassuring to a patient, who feels that their symptoms are 'real' and that they have been heard and understood. Population studies and the particularly Cnidian enterprise of statistics has given us valuable information on the behaviour of populations. We can therefore remain Cnidians while learning to become Coans. In the next chapter we will revisit the Cnidian camp. There are some very interesting conclusions that can be drawn about the behaviour of populations that are directly relevant to your blood pressure.

THIRTEEN

All in Together

We have discussed the large number of factors, known and unknown, that contribute to an individual having a heart attack. We have argued that by creating health using the techniques of Maharishi's Vedic Approach to Health, we should be able to spontaneously correct these factors, so that we could become healthy from inside out. The studies on Transcendental Meditation bear this out, but even if we follow this advice, there is another very curious factor that could at times work against the individual. We can state it thus: it is harder for any one individual to be perfectly healthy in a society which is generally unhealthy. To be sure, society is composed of individual people, but there is a dynamic link between each individual and the society he or she belongs to. It may seem surprising, but the more people who get sick, the harder it is for others to keep well. Conversely, the more people who get well, the harder it is for others to stay sick! If we want to achieve perfect health for ourselves, then we need to bring our fellow citizens along with us!

This may seem an unlikely concept. It implies that the fewer people who have high blood pressure in society, the harder it becomes for *anyone* to have high blood pressure. Or to put it another way, the closer

> ... the more people who get well, the harder it is for others to stay sick!

our average blood pressure is to optimum, the less likely it is that there will be people who have abnormally high blood pressure. Could it be that we affect each other so intimately that even our blood pressures are linked?

Surprising it may be, yet precisely this idea has been proposed by epidemiologists and experimentally tested by one of the most respected among them, the late Professor Geoffrey Rose. Professor Rose, with his colleague Professor Simon Day, reviewed data from the Intersalt study, the international multicentre study that we have met already in our discussion on the relationship between salt intake and hypertension. In all they looked at 52 different social groups who hailed from 32 countries. In each of these populations there were, as the authors put it: 'close and independent associations between the population mean and the prevalence of deviance for each of the variables examined'.[123] These variables included blood pressure.

> ... distributions of health-related characteristics move up and down as a whole ... The population thus carries a collective responsibility for its own health and well being, including that of its deviants.

So if someone in the community has high blood pressure, it is everyone's fault! By bringing our own blood pressure down, *even if we ourselves don't have high blood pressure*, we are actually helping our neighbour bring down his (or hers)! Conversely when our neighbour does something to help his blood pressure, ours improves as well! Improving the average blood pressure will move the *entire population towards normality*.

Rose and Day argue, as I have done in this book, against the dichotomy implied by the name hypertension. In reality no clear distinction exists; there is a smooth distribution of blood pressures from low to normal to high, in every population. They go further and argue against the dichotomy between normality and deviance in any sphere:

> It is commonly supposed that there is a clear distinction between normality and deviance whether the attribute is physiological (like blood pressure), behavioural (like eating or drinking), or social (like aggression). This view is attractive because it focuses attention on individuals who clearly have problems and at the same time reassures the majority: they are all right and not responsible for the deviant minority ... If normality and deviance are indeed

independent then the 'normal' majority are free to disapprove of the deviants. Heavy drinkers of alcohol are condemned, but moderation is beyond criticism. Obesity is bad, but average weight is socially acceptable (even in overweight populations). Football hooligans are deviant reprobates, but, in a market economy especially, less conspicuous aggression is usual and actually encouraged. In each case the population as a whole disowns the tail of its own distribution: hypertension, obesity, alcoholism and other behavioural problems can then be considered in isolation . . .

Rose and Day go on to imply that habits of eating and drinking spread contagiously among a population and affect some people more than others.

. . . but if the tail belongs to the distribution and the minority's problems exist as a consequence of the majority's attributes then it is no longer possible to regard normal (majority) behaviour as of no wider consequence. The way that most people eat, drink, and behave, even if it were harmless to themselves . . . may determine how many others, more vulnerable, will suffer as a consequence. *The health of society is integral* [my emphasis].

What this means essentially is that somehow the majority who have lower blood pressure drag down the blood pressure for the minority whose blood pressure might otherwise have been high!

Epidemiologists have used this argument to promulgate blanket diets for all. We should all eat less salt, and the problem of hypertension will disappear. While the reasoning is beguiling, as we have seen, it has led us into the trap of treating all human beings as if they were the same. We can achieve the desired effect of reducing average blood pressure in a much more refined way using our understanding of the doshas. The heavy, high-fat diet so popular in the West is far more detrimental to a Kapha than a Vata, who might actually thrive on it. Many authorities, having recognised that obesity is strongly correlated with heart disease, promote a low-fat, low-calorie diet. This suits those of Kapha tendency very well, but is too thin and unsustaining for the Vata who would feel most unhappy on it. Whereas before we had vulnerable Kaphas, we would now have contented Kapha and fragile Vata! Blanket diets, from the Vedic point of view, are almost as brutal as the 'carpet bombing' of a population with drugs. The answer is to give everyone the knowledge they need to become aware of their doshic make-up so that each can find a diet that suits him or her. You will recall that this was our second 'escape strategy' from the epidemiologist's dilemma. If it were carried out on a wide scale, then the average blood pressure in a community would approach normal and draw the hypertensive 'tail' of the distribution curve towards normal. The majority (of normotensives) would help the minority (of hypertensives).

That we all influence each other by talking to each other, by setting an example, by persuasion and by the constraints of societal mores is intuitively obvious. The idea that we interact collectively is developed to a much higher level in Maharishi's Vedic Approach to Health, and is explained in terms of consciousness. Talking, behaving, persuading and the customs of society all have their origin in thought. When we do something or say something, our action or our behaviour originates in a thought to say or do it. Thought, in turn, arises within our consciousness. In the Vedic outlook, our consciousness does not end at the edges of our brain or with our skin. Consciousness is seen as a field, rather like the familiar fields of gravity or electromagnetism, but deeper and more underlying. The field of consciousness referred to in Vedic Science corresponds to what in physics is called the Unified Field. In this outlook, we are not really separate from one another, we have a common source in consciousness. We could think of ourselves as being like waves on an ocean of consciousness. Each wave contributes to the state of the ocean as a whole.

Maharishi has pointed out that just as each individual has his or her consciousness, every grouping of individuals has its 'collective consciousness' as well. Think of the 'team spirit' that is generated in a football team, for example. A whole is created that seems to be greater than the sum of the individual parts. That group consciousness improves as people develop their own individual consciousness was originally suggested by Maharishi in the 1950s. He explains the concept of 'collective consciousness' as follows:

> Just as the consciousness of an individual determines the quality of his thought and behaviour, so also there exists another type of consciousness for a society as a whole; a collective consciousness for each family, city, state, or nation, having its own reality and the possibility of growth. The quality of the collective consciousness of a society is a direct and sensitive reflection of the level of consciousness of its individual members.[124]

Collective consciousness is a little bit like the air we breathe, in that we all have a responsibility to ensure its purity by not contributing pollutants. Any smoke that does emerge from an individual's fireplace affects us all. According to Maharishi, violence, negativity or conflict in society are the expressions of stress in collective consciousness. When the level of stress becomes sufficiently great, it bursts out into war, crime, accidents and disorder.

Some very significant studies, inspired by Maharishi, have shown that collective consciousness improves according to the numbers of people practising Transcendental Meditation in a community, especially if they are practising the more advanced technique, the TM-Sidhi programme.

These studies, carried out since the early 1970s, indicate that it may be possible for the 'minority to help the majority'. To improve the 'average level of consciousness' it may be necessary only to improve the individual consciousness of just a few. In 1976, crime rates were shown to improve when a relatively low percentage of a population (1 percent) began the practice of Transcendental Meditation.[125] The initial studies have been replicated including other indices of social malaise such as hospital admissions, traffic accidents and the like. The needed percentage of the total population to produce a positive effect appears to be much lower (the square root of 1 percent of the total population) if the subjects practise the more powerful TM-Sidhi programme.

Space does not allow a full exposition of this phenomenon about which books have been written. Suffice to say that such improvements have been measured and replicated many times, and are demonstrated in wide-ranging improvements in community life, for example by measuring lower negative indices such as crime rates, hospital admissions and war deaths, and higher positive indices such as measures of economic prosperity.[126]

So by practising Transcendental Meditation, you are not only helping your neighbour's blood pressure, you are also helping to protect him or her from the criminal element as well!

I am well aware that most people will be reading this book not because they wish to bring their neighbour's blood pressure down, or to improve the crime rate in their city, but because they want to do something to help themselves! This is perfectly valid thinking. Almost every one of the millions of people who practise the techniques of Maharishi's Vedic Approach to Health do so for personal reasons, to sleep better, have more energy during the day, improve their concentration or memory, get rid of tension headaches, improve their social life, or bring their blood pressure down. The next chapter gives you an overview on how you can do these things. However, in the light of this chapter you can have a warm glow, coming directly from the Cnidian campfire, that in doing something for yourself you are also doing something for your community as a whole.

FOURTEEN

Seven Steps to Perfect Health

Summary

1 Make sure you agree that your blood pressure really is too high.

2 If you are already taking drugs, and if blood pressure readings are satisfactory, then start 'stepping down' your drug therapy (always monitoring your blood pressure, and in consultation with your doctor).

3 Learn to transcend thought.

4 Start building up a picture of your doshic make-up and imbalances, with the help of a consultant in Maharishi's Vedic Approach to Health.

5 Become self-referral in your diet. Get in touch with what your body is asking for.

6 Tailor your daily routine to the circadian rhythms of the doshas and your particular doshic make-up. Take advantage of the other interventions offered within Maharishi's Vedic Approach to Health.

7 Monitor your blood pressure as you go.

How many times have you embarked with great good intentions on a new, healthier routine only to find that you have soon lost sight of your initial motivation? By going in detail into the decisions that modern medicine has taken on your behalf I hope I have given you the confidence to question them. I further hope that this will give you the impetus to take charge of your own welfare once and for all.

We have investigated the story behind the 'silent killer' and studied its history, its causation and its rise and fall as a medical 'disease'. We have seen that far from something 'fixed' that has got into us, an enemy to be shot at, hypertension is rather an imbalance in our body. It is moreover, a process that redefines itself minute by minute. High blood pressure is not like a rock, it changes. Since it is changing all the time why not give it a nudge in a direction that is more favourable to us?

This turns out to be easy. A key principle behind Maharishi's Vedic Approach to Health is the principle of least effort. Nature functions effortlessly to create a state of balance within itself. Balance is our natural state. Anything else is unnatural. As with a spinning top that is slightly off course, a nudge in the right direction may be all that is required to bring the body back to its naturally preferred course.

There are many ways to help nature recreate a healthy body. The first thing to remember is that you are doing wonderfully well already. Just to be alive is an incredible feat of nature. Trillions of chemical reactions, precisely timed and co-ordinated, are taking place just to allow you to be reading this page. While you are reading you are breathing, probably digesting, your heart is beating faithfully, your immune system fighting off viruses and eliminating dangerous cells from the blood. Makes you blink? Consider the simple act of blinking. To 'blink in sync', that is, for both eyes to move together in such a precisely co-ordinated way is a feat that would tax the resources of any robotics engineer who attempted to duplicate it in a machine. Yet we do it almost unconsciously, the entire process exquisitely managed by a myriad of natural laws that work 'behind the scenes', so effortlessly that we are not aware of them, only becoming aware of their enduring service when something goes wrong.

Looked at that way, it seems that things are going right most of the time. Our bodies are a part of the grand set of natural laws that govern the universe. These laws (some, but not all of which science has been able to express mathematically) do not operate randomly, but are orderly and intelligent. They work together and as a whole. Being part of nature means that we are a part of that whole, in fact we are an expression of it. If we are already functioning in accordance with millions of natural laws, why not harness a few more? We can bring ourselves into accordance with the totality of natural law if we know how. The techniques of Maharishi's Vedic Approach to Health, although profound and wise, are simple and fun! How could health care be fun? Western hospitals and doctors' surgeries do not spring to mind as fun places. These techniques are easy and enjoyable because nature does the work. As Hippocrates said: 'The physician merely applies the splint. Nature heals the broken bone.'

> If we are already functioning in accordance with millions of natural laws, why not harness a few more?

Remember my patient Brad whose blood pressure came down after he retired? The key to Brad's success was that he stopped doing a job he hated and that felt unnatural to him, and he started to do what gave him joy. You could say he started being true to himself. The techniques of Maharishi's Vedic Approach to Health are designed to help people function in accordance with the laws of nature deep within themselves, rather than conflict with them. It is much easier and much more delightful to catch the waves of nature's laws and surf them than to try and swim against them. In some very deep way, Brad reconnected himself to himself, and started surfing natural law!

Maharishi's Vedic Approach to Health gives us the ingredients we need to recreate Brad's success for ourselves. They point the way for you to be completely in tune with those myriads of natural laws that are effortlessly creating you. Then all the physical measurements we might care to make on your body are likely to be normal. The state of health yields a normal blood pressure. This does not work the other way around. Creating normal blood pressure does not guarantee the state of health.

Let's look at the seven steps in more detail.

1. *Make sure you agree that your blood pressure really is too high.* Get multiple readings from different people, including yourself, at different times of the day, over a period of four weeks. Make sure your blood pressure is measured on both arms on at least one occasion. Base your decisions for therapy on the arm that gives the highest readings and use that arm for subsequent measurements. Have three readings taken each time, discard the first and average the second and third. Get hold of a good-quality home monitoring device, so that you can take a few readings at home. If your home readings are much lower than those taken by professionals, discuss this with your doctor. You may be seeing the 'white coat' effect and 24-hour monitoring may be necessary. Otherwise, take the average over the whole four weeks of all the resulting readings to get a baseline figure.

If, at any point, you find your blood pressure is dangerously high, even on only one reading, say greater than 200/120, then you need to take drugs. Be guided by your doctor on this. This does not mean you cannot start creating health. Your health-creating methods can be working away in the background so that, before long, you can begin to 'step down' your drug therapy.

2. *If you are already taking drugs, consider a 'step-down' approach to reducing the dosage.* This can begin even before you get involved in alternatives, since you might be overmedicated. Working with your doctor, start reducing the dosage by small increments, monitoring the blood pressure every few days yourself and every week or so with your doctor or nurse. Then start creating health rather than side-effects by following steps 3 to 7.

3. *Learn the invaluable skill of transcending thought.* This may be all you need to do to bring your blood pressure into the normal range. To get behind one's thoughts and experience one's awareness in its simplest state is of inestimable value. For a long time the world thought it difficult or even impossible. Today for millions of people living in all parts of the world, it is a daily routine, as simple as brushing one's teeth.

People who practise Transcendental Meditation regularly report a marked reduction in stress and anxiety, increased levels of happiness and fulfilment, more stamina, energy and efficiency, better memory and concentration, increased calm and contentment, and relief from insomnia and tension headaches. More deeply refreshing and restoring than sleep or a long holiday, the single technique of Transcendental Meditation alone will prove to be an invaluable life-skill and help you in all aspects of your personal, family and professional life.

In my country, New Zealand, Transcendental Meditation is taught by a non-profit educational organisation and the structure is no doubt similar in other countries. This means that each country's organisation exists for the purpose of promoting Maharishi's teaching programmes, there are no shareholders and no profits taken at any level. The goals of Maharishi's organisation express the highest ideals for the good of mankind. In the early 1970s Maharishi outlined this vision for his organisation:

> We will count ourselves successful only when the problems of today's world are substantially reduced and eventually eliminated, and the health organisations of every country are capable of producing healthy individuals.

You cannot learn Transcendental Meditation from a book or from a videotape. Only a teacher who has practised Transcendental Meditation for years and has trained under Maharishi is able to teach you. Most cities have a centre for instruction in Transcendental Meditation. Look in the yellow pages for Transcendental Meditation as taught by Maharishi Mahesh Yogi. Or check some of the web-pages in the appendix to this book.

4. *Get an idea of what doshic imbalances are present*. Obviously if you have insomnia and lots of fears and worries, then Vata is the problem. Sometimes it is not so apparent which dosha is out of balance and it can often be more than one. Although there are books you can read, the doshas and their imbalances can be complex and confusing to the newcomer (especially when you consider that each dosha has five sub-doshas!), so the best way to get guidance on this is to see a consultant in Maharishi's Vedic Approach to Health. Your local Transcendental Meditation centre will be able to tell you if you have any resident

consultants, or when visiting consultants are planning to come to your area.

5. *Start eating appropriately as indicated by the promptings of your body.* When meal times come around, listen to what your body is telling you. If hunger is present, then you should eat. If hunger is not present, then the body is probably not ready for food just yet. You may even need to wait until the next meal time.

Trust your innate desires. If you feel like a piece of fruit cake, perhaps there is something in that cake you need! Try some, then notice whether you feel better or not. Temper this with your intellectual understanding of the doshas and with knowledge of the natural rhythms of the day. The midday meal, for example, is the most important and you should plan to be hungry for that. Follow the advice of your consultant in Maharishi's Vedic Approach to Health.

There are some general dietary recommendations from Maharishi's Vedic Approach to Health that can be made for everyone. They should nevertheless always be considered in the context of your doshic make-up.

- ❐ Avoid excessive amounts of oily or fatty foods, especially those of animal origin such as fatty meat, cream or cheese, as well as excessive amounts of salt. If Kapha dosha is predominant use low-fat milk, cheese and yoghurt; choose low-fat cuts of meat and cut visible fat off before cooking; don't eat the skin on chicken; grill or steam rather than fry. Use olive oil for salads and even as a substitute for butter, although a small amount of butter is acceptable. Those in whom Vata or Pitta are more predominant can be more relaxed about these recommendations than those who are strongly Kapha, since oily food in moderation is beneficial for Vata and to a lesser extent, Pitta.

- ❐ Salt is beneficial to Vata (although, as we have indicated, there is a point at which excessive salt is not good for anyone). If Kapha or Pitta are strongly present then salt should be avoided or taken in small quantities only. Remember that most salt we eat comes in processed foods (including bread and butter), so to really cut back on salt you need to find unsalted butter and other products as well as putting less salt on your food.

☐ Eat plenty of fresh fruit and vegetables of all kinds. Vata tends to be pacified to a greater extent by the heavier root vegetables, whereas Pitta and Kapha can favour more of the leafy green vegetables. Biscuits, pastries, sweets and takeaway foods should be taken only occasionally, particularly if Kapha is present in excess.

☐ If overweight, then you need to lose weight, but don't strain. Eating appropriately does not mean making ourselves miserable. Follow the advice of your consultant, and in particular follow your greatest ally, the advice of your body! Am I really hungry? Can I feel it? What is really going on (as opposed to what I thought was going on) in my stomach area?

☐ Avoid tea, coffee and carbonated drinks particularly if Vata is predominant, as these greatly exacerbate Vata. Avoid excessive amounts of alcohol. Alcohol raises blood pressure in the long term. Consider becoming a vegetarian, or at least cutting down on red meat.

☐ Let food be your medicine and medicine your food. In Maharishi's Vedic Approach to Health the distinction between medicine and food is less clear than in the West. Food, usually associated with nourishment only, also heals the body by pacifying the imbalanced doshas. Herbal food supplements provide nourishment as well as having a healing role. Consider taking a Maharishi herbal food supplement. Particularly if your cholesterol and lipid levels are high you should take the preparation known as Amrit Kalash. Your local consultant can recommend other suitable preparations for you. If you are a licorice fanatic and eating it in excess, then consider cutting back, since there is evidence that highly excessive amounts can raise blood pressure. In the Vedic system this would be related to its long-term effect in raising Kapha, leading to fluid retention, so those with Kapha predominance need to be more careful. When taken in moderation licorice is unlikely to cause harm and in fact is often used to good effect to pacify Vata and Pitta doshas.

6. *Tailor your daily routine to the circadian rhythms of the doshas.* Maharishi's Vedic Approach to Health gives many detailed instructions on how to conduct ourselves during the day for maximum fulfilment and well-being.

In general, we should avoid strain in our occupation and in our leisure. We should allow plenty of unstructured time to be with family and friends. The work hard, play hard ethic is risky to our health, if strain is involved. This does not mean that we should not enjoy the accomplishments of focused and vigorous work. It means that we should work with gusto until the point where we would start to strain. At that point we should back off and rest. We can tell when we have reached that point when work ceases to be fun and fails to hold our interest, or if we feel excessively tired when we stop work.

It is also necessary to find work that seems to come naturally to us, for this will yield the maximum rewards for least effort and strain. Once again you can use your knowledge of the doshas to find your niche. Those with a Kapha predominant constitution are best suited for heavy work requiring stamina and strength, or they may thrive in work that requires stability and a conservative outlook. Vata is usually associated with the type of work that requires creativity and fresh new ideas. Those who are predominant in Pitta are drawn towards entre-preneurial or managerial work. Thus, in a business, Vata might be found in the research and development sector, Pitta in the managerial and sales force, while Kapha would be represented by the accountants and bankers.

Similarly, Kapha sporting activities are those that require endurance and strength such as weightlifting. Pitta, being associated with heat, might be more suited to swimming, and Vata might feel more at home with a highly skilled recreation such as fencing or dancing, or may be satisfied by simply walking in pleasant surroundings. Exercise without strain is good for everyone. This does not necessarily mean joining a gym or investing in expensive equipment. Exercises based on Hatha Yoga (derived from the Veda) form an important part of Maharishi's Vedic Approach to Health. Forty minutes of brisk walking daily is excellent cardiovascular exercise. If you cannot afford the time, then try 'exercise snacking'. Take three or four minutes every hour or so to do some walking or stretching exercises. Any movement is better than none. You may not even need to leave your office!

A regular routine is important, especially if you have the Vata tendency to miss meals or get irregular sleep. 'Early to bed and early to rise' is an old maxim with which Maharishi's Vedic Approach to Health fully concurs.

If you are a smoker, then gently let go of the habit as your awareness grows through the regular experience of transcending thought. Many habits are the result of 'robotic' behaviour. For example, you might be talking to a friend on the telephone and be amazed to find three cigarette stubs in the ashtray at the end of the conversation. The first step in giving up smoking is to become an 'aware smoker'. Only when one is aware of what is *actually going on* is one even in a position to make more positive choices in behaviour. Your consultant in Maharishi's Vedic Approach to Health can help you with this.

Take advantage of the many other interventions offered within Maharishi's Vedic Approach to Health. These include powerful therapies such as Panchakarma, and approaches that come from other sections of the Veda such as Sthapatyaveda, the ancient science of architecture, that advises you how to build your house for better health! You can find out about when and where such services are offered by consulting the web-pages found in the appendix to this book.

7. *Keep monitoring, keep creating health.* Keep measuring your blood pressure from time to time, even when you feel sure that it has come down for good. The frequency of measurement depends on the degree of hypertension that has been present. If trying out a new therapy, in the presence of moderate elevation, then weekly monitoring is good, whereas if hypertension was mild or borderline and seems to have

responded to therapy, then monthly followed by three-monthly checks would be adequate. It is very important though, not to get complacent. Blood pressure can creep up. In the unlikely event that it reaches dangerous levels in spite of your best efforts, then do not be too proud to resume drug therapy, at least until it is back to safer levels.

Remember also, that it is not enough just to get blood pressure down, although it is a good start. At least your goal should be to put yourself in the best possible position to avoid having a heart attack or stroke, so other risk factors such as weight, smoking and stress levels should be monitored and improved. Your goal is to create health and overcome pragya aparadh. That means to reconnect yourself to the full potential of the natural laws that structure the mind and body so that you can enjoy perfect health, a life free from suffering, a life of enjoyment twenty-four hours per day. The Vedic tradition tells us we should accept nothing less.

To monitor that, remember your best guide is how you feel. Do I feel happy? Do I feel light and easy? In what areas do I feel discomfort? Don't settle for 'feeling more or less OK' or 'not unhappy anyway'. The human mind/body has infinite potential and happiness and fulfilment is your birthright.

In this book I have tried to give a deeper understanding of the story behind hypertension than that commonly presented as 'patient education'. Many of the ideas presented here have been overlooked or obscured by time. This has led the medical profession and the general public to blindly accept the pharmaceutical line. I have not wished here to downplay the dangers of hypertension. Cardiovascular diseases, along with cancer, are the scourges of our time. The 'silent killer' is aptly named. Yet when we examined the effects of 'fighting' it we found that we are fighting ourselves. The imbalance of hypertension is an imbalance within ourselves, a dislocation from that fundamental set of natural laws, the physicist's Unified Field, the underlying intelligence that informs us all.

We began with a consultation, one of millions of its kind. We examined the subtle and sometimes insidious pressures acting on doctor and patient alike. We saw that mainstream medicine, in which we have set such store, has made assumptions on our behalf, then forgotten all about them, and in doing so has forgotten about us.

We saw how, in a fragmented world, health care became disease treatment. We found that many doctors had galloped down the Cnidian pathway. The concept of health had become devalued, misunderstood and confused. Yet everything is inter-connected, and we followed this fruitful train of thought. Our natural state is oneness. When we fragment we create divisions that are unnatural. A society that forgets that, does so at its peril.

We returned to our roots, to the father of our Western medicine, Hippocrates, to find the crossroad at which medicine left us behind. We discovered the Coan school in which you, the patient, are appreciated for what you are, a unique and special person and not a standardised fragment. We traced the Coan thread back, culminating in the knowledge of the three doshas from Maharishi's Vedic Approach to Health.

We discovered the ancient body of knowledge, Vedic Science, whose currency is wholeness. We found that if we choose the path towards wholeness, by transcending thought, then the way is open for ease of life, happiness and health.

We turn our awareness one hundred and eighty degrees, transcend the habit of remaining uneasily within the boundaries of fragmented thought and experience the full potential of our inner intelligence directly. Transcending thought bridges the gaps and creates wholeness. We find balance in the body by developing our own inner balance. We create perfect blood pressure by creating perfect health.

Perfect health. Is it possible? In my practice, I have had the fulfilment of watching hundreds of patients recover from their illnesses using the techniques of Maharishi's Vedic Approach to Health. I feel enormously privileged to have had the opportunity to learn the rudiments of pulse diagnosis, to be able to teach the skill of transcending thought, to help people become self-referral in their diet and lifestyle, to organise Maharishi Panchakarma sessions, visits from highly skilled *Maharishi Vaidyas* (consultants in Maharishi's Vedic Approach to Health) and to encourage my patients to use all the techniques that I and others have learned from our training. Not only has blood pressure improved. I have looked on as arthritis symptoms dramatically eased, diabetes came under better control, eczema disappeared, dyspepsia was relieved, and depression and sleep problems became a thing of the past. On my files are patients who after years of vicious migraine headaches are now symptom-free. I have been able to take people off their drugs and have had the satisfaction of seeing patients take control of their health. Over the last 40 years millions of people in all parts of the world have benefited from Maharishi's Vedic Approach to Health. Doctors, teachers, company directors, scientists, housewives and sports people practise its techniques.

In his Vedic Approach to Health, Maharishi has brought together strands of ageless Vedic knowledge that had become scattered throughout India, Sri Lanka and Thailand. With the deep insight and wisdom that he received from his own teacher and the line of great Vedic Rishis who had preceded him, Maharishi has woven these precious filaments together to restore a magnificent tapestry of Vedic knowledge. Maharishi's Vedic Approach to Health cuts a swathe through the confused jungle of 'alternative medicines'. Its techniques are simple, effective, cost-effective and safe. They have stood the test of time and are quite robust enough to stand the tests of modern scientific scrutiny. Seek out your local Transcendental Meditation teachers. They can help you enormously.

Another level of satisfaction derives from teaching these techniques to people who profess to feel 'perfectly well'. To their delight they find themselves feeling even better than they ever thought possible. This proves to me once again that these techniques are here not simply to eradicate disease, lofty though that ideal may be. They are here to create the full potential of the healthy human being.

So I, for one, believe that perfect health is possible; that it is everyone's birthright to live in a state of ease, balance and orderliness in keeping with the natural laws inherent in our universe. Because we are all in this together, we may need to help each other along, but in the end I think it must be possible to create health in its perfection, because being healthy is easier than staying sick. It is much easier to push a swing at the right time. The universe moves in rhythms. The cycles of the seasons, the months and the days are echoed in the rhythms of our bodies. If you push a child's swing before it has quite reached you, you waste energy and you create unhappiness in the child. Once our awareness is sufficiently developed to listen to the body and respond to its cues in time, then like the swing, the body resonates to our actions. Perfect health flows as a natural result.

By telling you the story of hypertension, I hope you have realised, as I did when I met my patient Brad, that drug therapy is very often arbitrary and unnecessary. We can step out of that dance. I hope that you will feel inspired to take your health into your own hands.

I urge you not to have just a nice feeling about these ideas, but to actually take charge and create health for yourself as a living day-to-day experience. Your next step is to experience the benefits for yourself.

Cresswell Jones, now 48, is a much happier man. He enjoys meditating twice a day as does his wife, daughter and new son-in-law. His blood pressure is consistently around 135/85. His doshas are in balance and while his senses might not yet be full of bliss at all times, he is undoubtedly much more chipper than when we first met him. He was inspired to find that Quentin Frawley has been practising Transcendental Meditation for the last five years and that Brenda Finchley, their receptionist, also began a year ago. Damien Stent has not, but Cresswell no longer feels that his happiness swings on anything that Mr Stent does or thinks. Cresswell now divides his time between work, family, recreation and his local Transcendental Meditation centre for which he does the accounts. The only fly in the Cresswell ointment is the llama which has just butted through a fence and taken out the neighbour's winter brassica. The animal is clearly severely Vata deranged and Cresswell wonders vaguely whether, if the price was not excessive, he could arrange for the brute to have Panchakarma . . .

References

Note that reference is made more than once throughout the text to certain sources below.

1 Stason W. 'Opportunities to improve the cost-effectiveness of treatment for hypertension'. *Hypertension* 1991; 18 [suppl. I]: 161–6.

2 Aylett M. 'Pressure for change: Unresolved issues in blood pressure measurement'. *British Journal of General Practice* 1999; 49: 136–9.

3 Stewart M., Padfield P. 'Measurement of blood pressure in the technological age'. *British Medical Bulletin* 1994; 50 (2): 420–42.

4 Ramsay L., Williams B. et al. 'British Hypertension Society guidelines for hypertension management 1999: summary'. *British Medical Journal* 1999; 319: 630–5.

5 Guidelines Subcommittee. '1999 World Health Organization— International Society of Hypertension Guidelines for the Management of Hypertension'. *Journal of Hypertension* 1999; 17: 151–83.

6 Hansson L., Zanchetti A., et al. 'Effects of intensive blood-pressure lowering and low-dose aspirin in patients with hypertension: Principal results of the hypertension optimal treatment (HOT) randomised trial'. *The Lancet* 1998; 351: 1755–62.

7 Woodman R. Open letter disputes WHO hypertension guidelines. *BMJ* 1999; 318: 893.

8 Denton D. 'Can hypertension be prevented?' *Journal of Human Hypertension* 1997; 11: 563–9.

9 Rouse I., Beilin L. 'Blood pressure lowering effect of a vegetarian diet: Controlled trial in normotensive subjects'. *The Lancet* 1983; 1: 5–10.

10 Wallace R., Silver J. et al. 'Systolic blood pressure and long-term practice of the Transcendental Meditation and TM-Sidhi program: Effects of TM on systolic blood pressure'. *Psychosomatic Medicine* 1983; 45 (1): 41–6.

11 McCarron P., Smith G. et al. 'Blood pressure in young adulthood and mortality from cardiovascular disease'. *The Lancet* 2000; 355: 1430–1.

12 Jackson R. 'Guidelines on preventing cardiovascular disease in clinical practice' (editorial). *BMJ* 2000; 320: 659–61.

13 Hjemdahl P., Wiklund I. 'Quality of life on antihypertensive drug therapy: Scientific end-point or marketing exercise?' *Journal of Hypertension* 1992; 10: 1437–46.

14 McMahon S. 'Blood pressure and the risk of cardiovascular disease'. *New England Journal of Medicine* 2000; 342 (1): 50–2.

15 Rosengren A., Tibblin G. et al. 'Low systolic blood pressure and self perceived wellbeing in middle-aged men'. *BMJ* 1993; 306: 243–6.

16 Bou-Holaigah I., Rowe P. et al. 'The relationship between neurally mediated hypotension and the chronic fatigue syndrome'. *Journal of the American Medical Association* 1995; 274 (12): 961–7.

17 Payer L. *Medicine and culture: Notions of health and sickness in Britain, the U.S., France and West Germany*. London: Victor Gollanz, 1989.

18 Hay D. 'Cardiovascular disease in NZ, 1999: A summary of recent statistical information'. Heart Foundation Technical Report to Medical and Allied Professions 1999; 75: 1–20.

19 Moser M. 'Historical perspective on the management of hypertension'. *American Journal of Medicine* 1986; 80 (suppl. 5B): 1–11.

20 Bonita R., Beaglehole R. 'The decline in stroke mortality; the limited role of antihypertensive therapy'. *New Zealand Medical Journal* 1987; 100: 454–6.

21 Valtonene V. 'Role of infection in atherosclerosis'. *American Heart Journal* 1999; 138: S431–S433.

22 Seymour R., Steele J. 'Is there a link between peridontal disease and coronary artery disease?' *British Dental Journal* 1998; 184 (1): 33–8.

23 Ku C., Yang C. et al. 'Absence of a seasonal variation in myocardial infarction onset in a region without temperature extremes'. *Cardiology* 1998; 89 (4): 277–82.

24 Hu F., Willet W. et al. 'Snoring and risk of cardiovascular disease in women'. *Journal of the American College of Cardiology* 2000; 35 (2): 308–13.

25 van den Hoogen P., Feskens E. et al. 'The relation between blood pressure and mortality due to coronary heart disease among men in different parts of the world'. *N Engl J Med* 2000; 342 (1): 1–8.

26 Levy D., Larson M. et al. 'The progression from hypertension to congestive heart failure'. *JAMA* 1996; 275: 1557–62.

27 Moser M., Hebert P. 'Prevention of disease progression, left ventricular hypertrophy and congestive heart failure in hypertension treatment trials'. *J Am Coll Cardiol* 1996; 27: 1214–8.

28 Ferrara L., Raimondi, A. et al. 'Olive oil and reduced need for anti-hypertensives medications'. *Archives of Internal Medicine* 2000; 160: 837–42.

29 Appel L., Moore T. et al. 'A clinical trial of the effects of dietary patterns on blood pressure'. *N Engl J Med* 1997; 336 (16): 1117–24.

30 MacGregor G. 'Dietary sodium and potassium intake and blood pressure'. *The Lancet* 1983; 1: 750.

31 Sleight P. 'The importance of the autonomic nervous system in health and disease'. *Australian and New Zealand Journal of Medicine* 1997; 27: 467–73.

32 Emerson R. *Select Writings of Ralph Waldo Emerson*. London: Walter Scott, 1888: 86.

33 Bohm D. *Wholeness and the Implicate Order*. London: Routledge, 1980: 3.

34 Editorial. 'More on hypertensive labelling'. *The Lancet* 1985; 1 (8438): 1138–9.

35 Kawachi I., Wison N. 'The evolution of antihypertensive therapy'. *Social Science and Medicine* 1990; 31 (11): 1239–43.

36 Collins R., MacMahon S. 'Blood pressure, antihypertensive drug treatment and the risks of stroke and of coronary heart disease'. *British Medical Bulletin* 1994; 50 (2): 272–98.

37 Toyoshima H., Takahashi K. et al. 'The impact of side effects on hypertension management: A Japanese survey'. *Clinical Therapeutics* 1997; 19 (6): 1424–5.

38 Hilleman D., Ryschon K. et al. 'Fixed-dose combination vs monotherapy in hypertension: A meta-analysis evaluation'. *Journal of Human Hypertension* 1999; 13 (7): 477–83.

39 Steel N. 'Thresholds for taking antihypertensive drugs in different professional and lay groups: Questionnaire survey'. *BMJ* 2000; 320: 1446–7.

40 Sowers J., Bakris G. 'Antihypertensive therapy and the risk of type 2 diabetes mellitus'. *N Engl J Med* 2000; 342 (13): 969–70.

41 Jacobs D., Blackburn H. et al. 'Report of the conference on low blood cholesterol: Mortality associations'. *Circulation* 1992; 86: 1046–60.

42 Lindberg G., Bingefors K. et al. 'Use of calcium channel blockers and risk of suicide: Ecological findings confirmed in population based cohort study'. *BMJ* 1998; 316: 741–5.

43 Pahor M., Guralnik J. et al. 'Risk of gastrointestinal haemorrhage with calcium antagonists in hypertensive persons over 67 years old'. *The Lancet* 1996; 347: 1061–5.

44 Li Wan Po A. 'What lessons can be learnt from withdrawal of mibefradil from the market?' *The Lancet* 1998; 351: 1829–30.

45 Wright P. 'Untoward effects associated with practolol administration: Oculomucocutaneous syndrome'. *BMJ* 1975; 1: 595–8.

46 Hayton A. 'Practolol peritonitis with autopsy findings'. *New Zealand Medical Journal* 1978; 87: 177–9.

47 Brown A. *Observer*. Reprinted in *Christchurch Press* 3 December 1994.

48 Peay M., Peay E. 'The role of commercial sources in the adoption of a new drug'. *Social Science and Medicine* 1988; 73: 1183–9.

49 Avorn J., Chen M. et al. 'Scientific versus commercial sources of influence on the prescribing behaviour of physicians'. *American Journal of Medicine* 1983; 73: 4–8.

50 Wolfe S. 'Why do American drug companies spend more than \$12 billion a year pushing drugs? Is it education or promotion?' *Journal of General Internal Medicine* 1996; 11: 637–9.

51 Roughead E., Gilbert A. et al. 'Self-regulatory codes of conduct: Are they effective in controlling pharmaceutical representatives' presentations to general medical practitioners?' *International Journal of Health Services* 1998; 28 (2): 269–79.

52 Ziegler M., Lew P. et al. 'The accuracy of drug information from pharmaceutical sales representatives'. *JAMA* 1995; 273 (16): 1296–8.

53 Pickering T. 'Treatment of mild hypertension and the reduction of cardiovascular mortality: the "of or by" dilemma'. *JAMA* 1983; 249 (3): 399–400.

54 Skolbekken J. 'Communicating the risk reduction achieved by cholesterol reducing drugs'. *BMJ* 1998; 316: 1956–8.

55 Bodenheimer T. 'Uneasy alliance. Clinical investigators and the pharmaceutical industry'. *N Engl J Med* 2000; 342 (20): 1539–44.

56 Stelfox H., Getal C. 'Conflict of interest in the debate over calcium-channel anatagonists'. *N Engl J Med* 1998; 338: 101–6.

57 *From Compliance to Concordance: Achieving Shared Goals in Medicine*

Taking. London: The Royal Pharmaceutical Society of Great Britain, 1997.

58 Jachuck S., Brierley H. et al. 'The effect of hypotensive drugs on the quality of life'. *Journal of the Royal College of General Practitioners* 1982; 32: 103–5.

59 Finnerty F. 'Step-down therapy in hypertension'. *JAMA* 1981; 246 (22): 2593–6.

60 Lord Platt. 'Medical science: Master or servant'. *BMJ* 1967; 4: 440.

61 Editorial (editor's choice). 'Being smarter about preventing heart disease'. *BMJ* 2000; 320 (7236).

62 von Bertalanffy L. *General System Theory*. New York: George Braziller, 1968: 45.

63 Sedivy R. 'Chaodynamic loss of complexity and self-similarity cancer'. *Medical Hypotheses* 1999; 52 (4): 271–4.

64 Parker R., Doyle F. et al. 'A model-based algorithm for blood glucose control in type I diabetic patients'. *Transactions on Biomedical Engineering* 1999; 46 (2): 148–57.

65 Tomberg C. 'Focal enhancement of chaotic strange attractor dimension in the left semantic (Wernicke) human cortex during reading without concomitant change in vigilance level'. *Neuroscience Letters* 1999; 263 (2–3): 177–80.

66 Malek A., Alper S. et al. 'Hemodynamic shear stress and its role in atherosclerosis'. *JAMA* 1999; 282 (21): 2035–42.

67 Wagner C., Persson P. et al. 'Chaos in the cardiovascular system: An update'. *Cardiovascular Research* 1998; 40: 257–64.

68 Gastaldelli A., Mommoliti R. et al. 'Linear and nonlinear properties of heart rate variability: Influence of obesity'. *Annals of the New York Academy of Sciences* 1999; 879: 249–54.

69 Wagner C., Nafz B. et al. 'Chaos in blood pressure control'. *Cardio-vascular Research* 1996; 31: 380–7.

70 Kagiyama S., Tsukashima A. 'Chaos and spectral analyses of heart rate variability during head-up tilting in essential hypertension'. *Journal of the Autonomic Nervous System* 1999; 76: 153–8.

71 McWhinney I. *A Textbook of Family Medicine*. Oxford: Oxford University Press, 1981: 66.

72 Maharishi Mahesh Yogi. *Maharishi Forum of Natural Law and National Law for Doctors*. India: Age of Enlightenment Publications, 1995.

73 Maharishi Mahesh Yogi. *Enlightenment and Invincibility*. West Germany: Maharishi European Research University Press, 1978: 158.

74 Wallace R. *The Physiology of Consciousness*. Fairfield, Iowa: Maharishi International University Press, 1993.

75 Orme-Johnson D., Farrow J. (eds.) *Scientific Research on Maharishi's Transcendental Meditation and TM-Sidhi Programme* Vol. 1. New York: Maharishi European Research University, 1977.

76 Chalmers R., Clements G. (eds.) *Scientific Research on Maharishi's Transcendental Meditation and TM-Sidhi Programme* Vol 2–5. Netherlands: Maharishi European Research University, 1990–1996.

77 Wallace R., Benson H. et al. 'A wakeful hypometabolic physiologic state'. *American Journal of Physiology* 1971; 221: 795–9.

78 Epply K., Abrams A. et al. 'Differential effects of relaxation techniques on trait anxiety: A meta-analysis'. *Journal of Clinical Psychology* 1989; 45: 957–74.

79 Alexander C., Rainforth M. et al. 'Transcendental Meditation, self-actualization and psychological health: A conceptual overview and statistical meta-analysis'. *Journal of Social Behaviour and Personality* 1991; 6: 189–247.

80 Chrousos G., Gold P. 'The concepts of stress and stress system disorders'.

JAMA 1992; 267 (9): 1244–52.

81 Beilin L. 'Stress, coping, lifestyle and hypertension: A paradigm for research, prevention and non-pharmacological management of hypertension'. *Clinical and Experimental Hypertension* 1997; 19 (5 & 6): 739–52.

82 Mario T., Verdecchia P. et al. 'Age and blood pressure changes: A 20-year follow-up study in nuns in a secluded order'. *Hypertension* 1988; 12: 457–61.

83 Everson S., Kaplan G. et al. 'Hypertension incidence is predicted by high levels of hopelessness in Finnish men'. *Hypertension* 2000; 35: 561–7.

84 Cottington E., Matthews K. 'Occupational stress, suppressed anger and hypertension'. *Psychosomatic Medicine* 1986; 48 (3/4): 249–60.

85 Eisenberg D., Delbanco T. 'Cognitive behavioural techniques for hypertension: Are they effective?' *Annals of Internal Medicine* 1993; 118: 964–72.

86 Orme-Johnson D., Walton K. 'All approaches to preventing or reversing effects of stress are not the same'. *American Journal of Health Promotion* 1998; 12(5): 297–9.

87 Schneider R., Staggers F. et al. 'A randomized controlled trial of stress reduction for hypertension in older African Americans'. *Hypertension* 1995; 26: 820–7.

88 Alexander C., Schneider R. et al. 'Trial of stress reduction for hypertension in older African Americans II. Sex and risk subgroup analysis'. *Hypertension* 1996; 28: 228–37.

89 Herron R., Hillis S. et al. 'The impact of the Transcendental Meditation program on government payments to physicians in Quebec'. *American Journal of Health Promotion* 1996; 10(3): 208–16.

90 Barnes V., Treiber F. et al. 'Acute effects of Transcendental Meditation on hemodynamic functioning in middle-aged adults'. *Psychosomatic Medicine* 1999; 61: 525–31.

91 Alexander C., Robinson P. et al. 'The effects of Transcendental Meditation compared to other methods of relaxation and meditation in reducing risk factors, morbidity, and mortality'. *Homeostasis* 1994; 35 (4–5): 243–63.

92 Orme-Johnson D. 'Medical care utilization and the Transcendental Meditation program'. *Psychosomatic Medicine* 1987; 49: 493–507.

93 Barnes V., Schneider R. et al. 'Stress, stress reduction, and hypertension in African Americans: An updated review'. *Journal of the National Medical Association* 1997; 89: 464–76.

94 Alexander C., Barnes V. et al. 'A randomized controlled trial of stress reduction on cardiovascular and all cause mortality: A 15 year follow-up on the effects of Transcendental Meditation, mindfulness and relaxation'. *Circulation* 1996; 93: 629. Abstract.

95 Cunningham C., Brown S. et al. 'Effects of Transcendental Meditation on symptoms and electrographic changes in patients with cardiac syndrome X'. *American Journal of Cardiology* 2000; 85: 653–5.

96 Castillo-Richmond A., Schneider R. et al. 'Effects of stress reduction on carotid atherosclerosis in hypertensive African Americans'. *Stroke* 2000; 31: 568–73.

97 Nalepka J., Callahan S. *Capsized.* Auckland: HarperCollins, 1992.

98 Ramsay L., Yeo W. et al. 'Non-pharmacological therapy of hypertension'. *British Medical Bulletin* 1994; 50 (2): 494–508.

99 Elliott P., Stamler J. et al. 'Intersalt revisited: Further analyses of 24 hour sodium excretion and blood pressure within and across populations'. *BMJ* 1996; 312: 1249–53.

100 Godlee F. 'The food industry fights for salt' (editorial). *BMJ* 1996; 312: 1239–40.

101 Richards M., Nicholls G. et al. 'Blood-pressure response to moderate sodium restriction and to potassium supplementation in mild essential hypertension'. *The Lancet* 1984; 757–61.

102 Crookshank F. 'Theory of Diagnosis'. *The Lancet* 1926; 939–99.

103 Dixon A. 'Family medicine—at a loss for words?' *Journal of the Royal College of General Practitioners* 1983; 33: 358–63.

104 Chichester F. *The Lonely Sea and the Sky*. London: Hodder and Stoughton, 1964.

105 Guyatt G., Sacket D. et al. 'Determining optimal therapy—randomized trials in individual patients'. *N Engl J Med* 1986; 314: 889–92.

106 Jeans, J. *The Mysterious Universe*. Cambridge: Cambridge University Press, 1930: 148.

107 Eddington, A. *The Nature of the Physical World*. Ann Arbor: University of Michigan Press, 1974: 276.

108 Broadbent W. 'The pulse: Its diagnostic, prognostic, and therapeutic indications'. *The Lancet* 1875; 2: 901–7.

109 Hawthorne C. 'The sphygmomanometer and the sphygmograph in relation to the measurement of arterial blood pressures'. *The Lancet* 1911; 1: 424–8.

110 Kasture H. *Concept of Ayurveda for Perfect Health and Longevity*. Nagpur, India: Shree Baidyanath Ayurveda Bhavan Ltd, 1991.

111 Mansfield P. *Healthy Scepticism: a Second Opinion on Drug Promotion for NZ GPs*. Wellington: Medical Lobby for Appropriate Marketing Inc, 1998; 1.

112 Leiter L., Abott. et al. 'Canadian recommendations on the nonpharmacological treatment of hypertension: Recommendations on obesity and weight loss'. *Canadian Medical Association Journal* 1999; 160 (9 suppl.): S7–S12.

113 Bean L. 'Dairy products: Emerging health benefits'. *Dialogue* (Newsletter of Dairy Advisory Bureau, New Zealand) 1999; (32) 1–5.

114 MacLean D., Chockalingam A. et al. 'Elevated blood cholesterol and the prevention of heart disease'. *Canadian Journal of Cardiology* 1999; 15 (4): 407–8.

115 Kritchevsky D. 'Diet and atherosclerosis'. *American Heart Journal* 1999; 138: S426–S430.

116 Sundaram V., Hanna A. et al. 'Inhibition of low-density lipoprotein oxidation by oral herbal mixtures Maharishi Amrit Kalash-4 and Maharishi Amrit Kalash-5 in hyperlipidemic patients'. *American Journal of Medical Science* 1997; 314 (5).

117 Schneider R., Nidich S. 'Lower lipid peroxide levels in practitioners of the Transcendental Meditation program'. *Psychosomatic Medicine* 1998; 60: 38–41.

118 Magarian G. 'Reserpine: A relic from the past or a neglected drug of the present for achieving cost containment in treating hypertension?' *Journal of General Internal Medicine* 1991; 6: 561–72.

119 Sharma H. *Freedom from Disease*. Toronto, Ontario: Veda Publishing Inc., 1993: 186.

120 Boivin J. Quoted in: Oliver D. *Fractal Vision*. Indiana, USA: Sams Publishing, 1992: 216.

121 Royer A. 'The role of the Transcendental Meditation technique in promoting smoking cessation: A longitudinal study'. *Alcoholism Treatment Quarterly* 1994; 11: 221–38.

122 Bhishagranta, K., ed. *The Sushruta Samhita*. Varanasi, India: Chowkhamba Sanskrit Series Office, 1981: 140.

123 Rose G., Day S. 'The population mean predicts the number of deviant individuals'. *BMJ* 1990; 301: 1031–4.

124 Maharishi Mahesh Yogi. Foreword. In: *Scientific Research on Maharishi's Trancendental Meditation and TM-Sidhi Programme.* Vol. 1. New York: Maharishi European Research University, 1977: 2.

125 Borland C., Landrith G. 'Improved quality of city life through the Transcendental Meditation program: Decreased crime rate'. In: *Scientific Research on Maharishi's Trancendental Meditation and TM-Sidhi Programme.* Vol. 1. New York: Maharishi European Research University, 1977: 639–48.

126 Hagelin J. *Manual for a Perfect Government.* Fairfield, Iowa: Maharishi University of Management Press, 1998.

Useful Web-Pages

Perfect Blood Pressure

If you have enjoyed reading this book, then check this website for new and related information.
www.perfectbloodpressure.com

Transcendental Meditation

Sites for other countries can be accessed using the links provided within these sites.

Germany — www.netlink.de/tm
Israel — www.netvision.net.il/php/ims
Netherlands — www.tm.nl
New Zealand — www.tm.org.nz
freephone: 0800 ENJOYTM
(0800 365 698)
Spain — www.maharishiveda.com
Sweden — www.miki.a.se
United Kingdom — www.transcendental-meditation.org.uk
telephone 08705 143733
United States of America — www.tm.org

Scientific Research on Transcendental Meditation

Maharishi European Research University in Germany — www.netlink.de/meru/
Maharishi Vedic Universities in the United States — www.maharishi.org
Center for Natural Medicine and Prevention (Dr Schneider) — www.mum.edu/CMVM
www.mum.edu/CNMP

Consciousness-based Education

Maharishi University of Management — www.mum.edu
Maharishi Corporate Development program — www.tm.org/mcdp

Related Medical Site

British Medical Journal — www.bmj.com
Carries frequent articles on hypertension. Their CiteTrack Alert service can email you when a new article appears. Full text on-line.

Acknowledgements

I must first express my deepest gratitude to Maharishi Mahesh Yogi whose extraordinary contribution to the happiness and well-being of mankind, and whose profound insights, have been an enduring inspiration to me since I first encountered his work thirty years ago.

I would next like to thank my family, my wife Sally and our children Cris, Holly and Toby for their forbearance and support as this book went through its many incarnations.

I wish also to thank those people who have reviewed the manuscript, made suggestions and selflessly lent their time. In particular I am deeply grateful to Dr Deborah Hankey for her excellent contributions, encouragement and many hours spent editing and thinking creatively on my behalf; Gill Sanson for her constant support from the very early stages of the project; Dr Byron Rigby for his enthusiasm and invaluable suggestions; Dr Gary Nicholls, Editor of the *New Zealand Medical Journal*, for his valuable comments on the medical aspects of the text, and Bryan Lee for his astute comments, as well as those of Dr Hari Sharma, Dr David Nicholls, Graeme Lodge, Neil Hamill, John Hodgson and John Bird. I must also thank my hardworking staff and colleagues who kept Hillmorton Medical Centre afloat during my writing absences. In particular I must acknowledge Dr Marise Brice for her interest in the project and for her extremely generous support in covering my surgery sessions, without which the time would not have been available for me to complete the book. My thanks also to Penelope Donovan for her illustrations and to the staff of Otago and Canterbury Medical Libraries for their diligence in tracing references and illustrations. Finally, I wish to warmly acknowledge Bernice Beachman and Philippa Gerrard of Penguin Books (NZ) Ltd for their confidence in me as a first-time author and their good-humoured help in guiding me through the publishing process. To all these people, and the many more who have given their support, my heart-felt thanks.

INDEX